Lovely LANDSCAPE QUILTS

USING STRINGS & SCRAPS TO PIECE AND APPLIQUÉ SCENIC QUILTS

Cathy Geier

Fons&Porter
CINCINNATI, OHIO

Table of Contents

Introduction

Using strips to create landscapes is a topic as high as the skies and as broad as the Western plains—there are so many methods! Many of us are undoubtedly aware of the jelly roll quilt phenomenon: Start with a roll of strips, sew, and within a short time you have a small quilt top. Well, what happens when we take more time and give more thought to our strip selection? Gorgeous landscape quilts can be the result. Some of these quilts can be fairly complicated with the challenge of intricate piecing, while others can be beautifully simple and easy with no piecing required.

In this book, I hope to introduce you to new ideas for using scraps and leftover fabric strips. If you have strip pieced or string pieced quilts before, you know how easy the sewing can be. If you like the look of strip-pieced landscapes but you don't have the time or patience for sewing strips, I will show you ways to put these quilts together without piecing. If you like the idea of quickly piecing colorful blocks and arranging them into landscapes, there is help for you here too. And lastly, if you like the look of long, perfectly straight strips, this book will show you how to achieve those perfect results using a tear-away foundation.

In other chapters, I'll show you some easy ways to create and add embellishments to your strip-pieced quilts. I'll show you how you can create steep mountains or gently rising ground by simply changing the angle at which you sew your strips together. I'll show you how to combine your batiks and prints to create skies and water. There are some very simple things you can do with strips from your own stash to create beautiful art quilts.

LET'S GET STARTED!

CHAPTER 1

THE Amazing STRIP!

*An endless variety of
strip-pieced landscapes
from contributing artists*

So many landscapes, so little time! (Or is it "So many landscapes, sew little time?") If you're like me, you want to try making different kinds of quilts. You can create an endless variety of quilts simply by using straight strips of fabric.

Take a look at some of the wonderful art quilts in the following pages. All of the quilts in this chapter are made using strips of fabric. If you page through the projects chapter of the book, you'll see that I put landscapes together using fabric strips, but I'm only one of many artists who use this method to create their artwork.

Let's take a closer look at some of the many styles of landscapes and see how the artists used strips of fabric to create their landscape quilts. Some of the following quilts are pieced, and some are fused together using fusible interfacing or glue sticks to anchor the strips to a foundation. In this book, I'll show you how to do both techniques while teaching you different ways to turn your scraps into art.

RAINBOWS OF SUMMER (DETAIL)
by Ann Brauer | 96" × 96" (243.8cm × 243.8cm)
Photographed by John Polak

Reta Budd

ABUNDANCE
by Reta Budd | 38" × 18" (96.5cm × 45.7cm)
Photographed by Sheila Dunbar

Reta Budd is from Canada and is a member of several quilt groups, including the Fibre Arts Group and the Oxford Quilters. She has exhibited her quilts throughout Canada, the United States, Japan and England. Reta's quilts have been accepted in national and provincial juried shows where she has won many awards. She spent a few years oil painting and has sewn most of her life, but she didn't start landscape quilting until the mid-1990s. Though she has taken a few art classes here and there, Reta describes herself as being self-taught. Now, she teaches others. Why does she choose the fabric medium to express herself? Because like us, she loves the feel and texture of fabric. Reta calls her landscapes "soulscapes." She writes that "nature nourishes my soul" and hopes that her landscapes "convey this spiritual depth to the observer."

Reta's quilt, *Abundance*, captures the scene of wheat fields in the fall and the wide-open spaces of the prairie under stormy skies. I've driven though the southern Alberta and Saskatchewan provinces, and she has captured the lonely beauty and isolation of the landscape. The use of deep, stormy sky fabric hints toward the coming winter in all its harshness and adds to the moody beauty of her scene.

Reta's strip-pieced landscapes are backdrops for her extensive embellishment. In the detail photograph of *Abundance*, you can see how she uses yarns, stitching and thread to create the wonderful texture of her landscape.

ABUNDANCE (DETAIL)
Photographed by Dave Knox

Coreen Zerr

Coreen Zerr hails from Canada and is passionate about making strip-pieced quilts. She comes from a traditional quilting background but got hooked on landscape quilting twenty years ago after making her first strip-pieced landscape. Coreen teaches others now and sells commissioned landscape quilts throughout Canada. After all these years of strip piecing, Coreen says that using strips is still her favorite way to depict sky and water scenes and to create backgrounds for thread painting.

Much of her inspiration comes from her surroundings, the sunrises and sunsets over the Strait of Georgia where she lives, and the farm on which she was raised.

In her quilt *Manitoba Homecoming*, notice the warm, soft sky and the way her use of soft, muted colors throughout the quilt welcomes you into the scene—she has created a feeling of nostalgia. Coreen designed the quilt using the farmhouse she grew up in and her father-in-law's barn. According to Coreen, because every farm in Manitoba has a slough, "There must be something rusting away in the bush, and sunflowers are a common crop." Coreen and her sister-in-law put this quilt together, adding appliqué to the pieced quilt top. Not surprisingly, it has won awards throughout the United States and Canada.

MANITOBA HOMECOMING
by Coreen Zerr and Phyllis Gagne | 77½" × 86½" (196.9cm × 219.7cm)
Photographed by Coreen Zerr

MANITOBA HOMECOMING (DETAIL)
Photographed by Coreen Zerr

Ann Brauer

Artist Ann Brauer uses pieced strips in a bold and dramatic way. Ann comes from a sewing background, having grown up on a farm surrounded by her grandmother's quilts. She joined 4-H where she made clothes for herself and, eventually, costumes for her school's plays. As a young woman, she pursued a career in law, becoming a successful attorney and owning her own company. Then *it* happened—in Ann's own words, "I realized if I made quilts, I could buy fabric." (A marvelous revelation!) Soon she quit her job, moved to western Massachusetts and began supporting herself by her quilting art. Ann is a self-taught artist.

"I feel compelled to make my quilts, which explore the use of color, fabric and the traditions of quilt making to create feelings of space and place," she writes. Many of her quilts reflect the prairies where she grew up and the "endless possibilities that the horizons offer." Ann's quilts are visual feasts of color. Using blocks of painterly arranged values and colors, she creates landscapes with horizon lines, water and skies. Her blocks of color are pieced using a quilt-as-you-go technique, and then they are arranged and joined together. Each quilt is complete at that stage—she adds no appliqué.

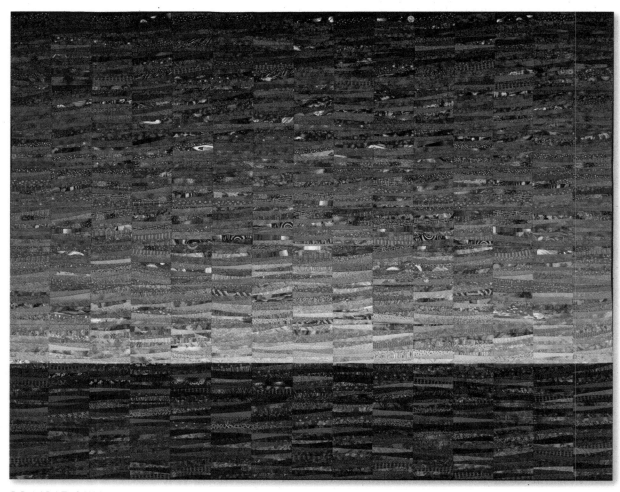

PRAIRIE SKY
by Ann Brauer | 96" × 120" (243.8cm × 304.8cm)
Photographed by John Polak

As you look at Ann's quilts, notice how she introduces fabrics of light values into her gradated and ever-deepening colored blocks. These flecks of light and color give her quilts dimension and sparkle. They suggest sunlight, starlight or reflections of moonlight on the water. Though the five quilts shown here feature particularly vibrant colors, Ann uses many different color combinations to create her quilts. I highly recommend reading her blog (see Resources on page 125) to see the new and different combinations she creates. You can learn marvelous things about color by studying her quilting palette.

MOONLIGHT
by Ann Brauer | 45" × 45" (114.3cm × 114.3cm)
Photographed by John Polak

RAINBOWS OF SUMMER

by Ann Brauer | 96" × 96" (243.8cm × 243.8cm)
Photographed by John Polak

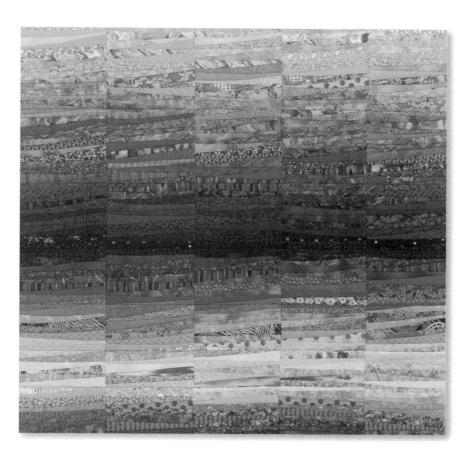

RAINBOWS OF AUTUMN
by Ann Brauer | 45" × 45" (114.3cm × 114.3cm)
Photographed by John Polak

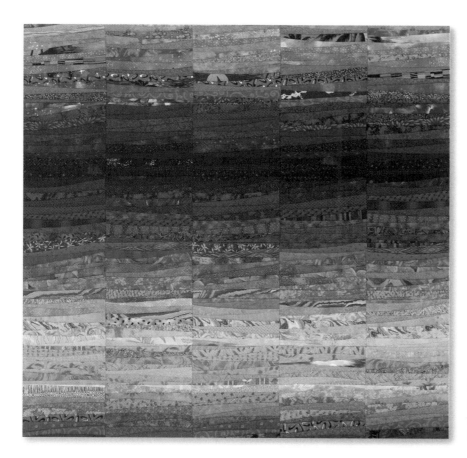

RAINBOWS OF DAWN
by Ann Brauer | 45" × 45" (114.3cm × 114.3cm)
Photographed by John Polak

Karen Reese Tunnell

Strips can also be used to form specific elements in the landscape. Karen Tunnell uses strips to create everything from rocks to the ridges of trees.

Karen's father was a landscape painter, and his work was a great inspiration to Karen because it influenced the way she looks at foregrounds, backgrounds, texture and color. For Karen, working with strips of fabric is a lot like developing a painting with brushstrokes. "It's very impressionistic," she writes. Karen finishes her landscapes with some hand coloring, using fabric markers or colored pencils to create depth and to blend fabrics. Her quilt *My Boulders* is a view of a rocky path down to Lake Santeetlah in western North Carolina where her family has a home.

Karen has a wonderful way of putting these quilts together: She sews strips directly to the batting and arranges her individual landscape elements in an almost mosaic picture style, often leaving herself plenty of room for embellishment with hand embroidery, knitting, painting and appliqué. If you look closely, you'll notice she uses all kinds of fabrics, from batiks to prints, to create her highly textured scenes. Once she develops "areas of color," she hand sews them together to form the larger landscape.

Cherohala Boulders was inspired by a photograph of a rock outcropping alongside a highway.

MY BOULDERS
by Karen Reese Tunnell | 24" × 48" (61cm × 121.9cm)
Photographed by Photography Center of Atlanta

CHEROHALA BOULDERS
by Karen Reese Tunnell | 31" × 50" (78.7cm × 127cm)
Photographed by Photography Center of Atlanta

Elena Stokes

Elena Stokes uses strips of fabric in marvelous ways to create sunlit reflections in the water or to create soft landscapes in blues and green. Her contemporary quilts are soft and representational in nature, yet still have the feeling of modernity. Her strips of fabric are torn, fused and stitched. The tearing adds additional texture and dimension to her landscapes.

Elena describes her artistic training as coming from observation, reading, "plain, old-fashioned trial and error" and "just doing it." I believe many of us are too afraid to "just do it." We get nervous and feel insecure when we step out of our comfort zones to try something new. The way Elena approaches her art is very inspiring.

Working more intuitively, Elena does not create her landscapes with specific places in mind. Rather, she tries to capture "a feeling of somewhere." She plays with color and texture for the sheer joy of working the design and creating a mood. This is evident in her quilt *Tranquil Marsh—Wild Iris* and its soothing palette of blues and greens.

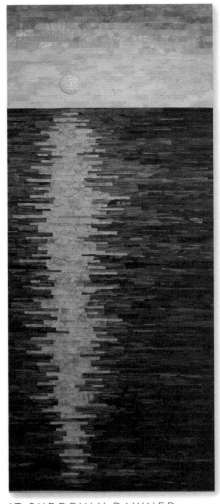

TRANQUIL MARSH—WILD IRIS
by Elena Stokes | 78" × 32" (198.1cm × 81.3cm)
Photographed by Elena Stokes

IT SUDDENLY DAWNED
by Elena Stokes | 75½" × 32" (191.8cm × 81.3cm)
Photographed by Elena Stokes

Denise Labadie

POULNABRONE DOLMEN
by Denise Labadie | 32" × 63" (81.3cm × 160cm)
Photographed by Esmond Snell

Unlike Elena's nonspecific landscapes, Colorado artist Denise Labadie chooses very specific places and objects to recreate in strips of fabric. By using her own hand-painted stone fabrics, she strives to create maximum realism in her stone monuments while surrounding them with abstract skies and earth. For Denise, "the landscape is key to providing the context of Irish place, spirit and timelessness." Her quilts reflect her deep "connection with ancient stones and ruins."

Denise's careful use of color and shading combines with the subtle textures in her standing stones to give her fabric monuments a larger-than-life mysticism untouched by time.

Denise has a sewing background; she made her own clothes and had precision sewing drilled into her at a young age through her involvement with 4-H. She began quilting nearly thirty years ago and took her first art quilt class in 1993. She traveled to Ireland in 1994, where she was immediately and inexorably drawn to the great standing stones.

Since her foray into art quilting, Denise's work has evolved. Having little visual art training in her past, she learned perspective and lighting through classes and by working with other quilters. She describes herself as having to confront a lifelong fear of these two things! Her quilts are created with multiple strips of fabric, yarn and trims. Yet they serve as visual storyboards, highlighting her stone encounters, their ancient stories and the wonderment she feels in their presence.

POULNABRONE DOLMEN (DETAIL)
Look carefully and notice how Denise uses various yarns in her landscape to add texture and color.
Photographed by Esmond Snell

15

Kathy Schattleitner

Kathy Schattleitner has made traditional quilts off and on for twenty years. Eventually she became bored with the precision piecing required of traditional block making and discovered the "freedom of using strips of fused fabric to depict natural forms and shapes."

Canyonlands is a wonderful example of the use of carefully arranged strips to create an open, flowing landscape. Kathy captures the beauty and expansiveness of the Southwestern deserts through a carefully thought-out design and the use of fused fabric strips. Like many other artists mentioned in this book, she does not have a background in the visual arts. In fact, when she grew up in England, art making of any type was considered a waste of time!

CANYONLANDS
by Kathy Schattleitner | 19¾" × 33" (50.2cm × 83.8cm)
Photographed by Franklin Nored

Marjan Kluepfel

California artist Marjan Kluepfel is a member of the California Fiber Artists, the Studio Art Quilt Associates, the Northern California Quilt Council and the Surface Design Association. Oil and watercolor painting was her hobby when she was growing up in the Netherlands. Her training, however, is in microbiology! When she moved to the United States, Marjan discovered quilting. Twenty-five years later, she uses fabric and thread instead of paper and paint, and "a sewing machine instead of a brush." She rarely plans out her quilts; instead, she loves to create her pieces spontaneously—just for fun! Her quilts certainly reflect her love of nature and all its wonders.

A Year in the Forest was created by sewing twelve different fabric strips together, each fabric representing one month of the year. Grays were used for winter months, greens for the spring and summer, and browns for the fall. Batik trunks were fused on top and free-motion quilted. To this simple but lovely quilt top, Marjan added leaves.

Redwoods was also created by fusing multiple thin strips of fabric to create trees. In this case, she placed strips of fabric on a fusible web foundation, creating tree trunks out of multiple strips of brown batiks and hand-dyed fabric. Marjan used the raw edges to create the beautiful texture of redwood tree trunks.

REDWOODS
by Marjan Kluepfel | 29" × 49 " (73.7cm × 124.5cm)
Photographed by Marjan Kluepfel

A YEAR IN THE FOREST
by Marjan Kluepfel | 63" × 40" (160cm × 101.6cm)
Photographed by Marjan Kluepfel

Designing WITH STRIPS!

Thoughts on inspiration, fabrics and design

I'm the kind of quilter who jumps in and figures out what to do once I'm in the water. My first strip-pieced quilt was *Lover's Leap*. I picked a tricky design to whet my skills, but when inspiration hits, I jump first and ask questions later. You may not be this kind of person, and that is just fine—and mighty sensible of you! If I have given you lots of ideas and piqued your interest with all those beautiful quilts in the first chapter, then there are a few more things to work out before you jump. If you still need specific inspiration, this chapter can help you, too.

LOVER'S LEAP

59" × 48" (149.9cm × 121.9cm)
Created out of all kinds of fabrics, including batiks, this was my first strip-pieced landscape. My inspiration was the rock formation along the Pictured Rocks National Lakeshore in Michigan's Upper Peninsula.

Finding Inspiration

Many resources are available to help you visualize and create a landscape with your own strips of fabric. My favorite place to get inspired is Google images. Use your favorite search engine to look for pictures of sunsets, ocean shores, deserts, forests and more. The earth around us is one of the best sources of inspiration, and photographs are plentiful. Before we continue, though, I need to explain an aspect of copyright law.

As long as you do not directly copy an artist's work, and you use the images only for general ideas regarding color choices and themes, you will not be violating copyright laws. Copyright laws are violated if you use another's image and directly imitate it; in that case, your quilt is a "derivative" of another person's artwork, even if you are, for example, creating a quilt from a painting.

I violated copyright law when I made my quilt *Poppies in the Rain and Mud* in imitation of the painting *Field Poppies* without permission from the artist, Wendy Kroeker. When I discovered my error, I contacted her. Wendy was gracious enough to allow me to not only show this quilt, but to give me permission to show you how you can recreate it, too. If you would like to use another artist's image in such a way, you must ask them for permission first. Ask, even if you don't think you would ever display it. Most artists will be flattered and curious to see what you can create using their art as inspiration.

There will be times when you want to make something but simply can't figure out where to start. One way to approach the "what to make" problem is to look at your stash of fabric. What do you have the most of? If you have lots of blues, look for water scenes that inspire you. If you have a large selection of beiges and tans, perhaps a desert is in your future. If you have a lot of green fabric, think of forests or meadows. You can always pick up a few quarter yard pieces of fabric to augment your creation as needed.

Learning the Hard Way

I learned about copyright law the hard way when I made the quilt *Poppies in the Rain and Mud*, shown here (top). I was inspired by the painting called *Field Poppies* by Wendy Kroeker (bottom).

Choosing Fabrics

How do you know if your fabrics will work? Cut out a strip! There are no hard-and-fast rules when picking out fabrics. The only guideline is to avoid putting a wider solid or tone-on-tone strip in with other strips of a different texture, or vice versa. I once heard a discussion at a cutting counter about whether batiks should be combined with regular cotton prints. My answer is "Yes!" In strip-pieced quilts, I combine them all the time.

Another consideration you might take into account as you decide what to create are the types of scraps in your stash. Are your remnants long? Do you have lots of 8"–10" (20.3cm–25.4cm) scraps of fabric? If you want to use up all of those small pieces, perhaps you should think about string piecing a patchwork background and appliquéing landscape elements on top. Conversely, long fabric lengths lend themselves to sweeping landscapes.

Color and texture matter more than the type of fabric. Feel free to mix all kinds of fabric.

After you decide on the scene you'd like to create, gather your fabrics. Arrange each color by value from darkest to lightest. For the most part, the darkest value fabrics will be used in the foreground. I find a value-finding tool incredibly helpful with this process. (Cottage Mills makes a set that comes in green and red so you can see the value of your fabrics throughout the color spectrum.) As you design, think more about value and less about color. For example, look at the shadowed area under the arch in *Lover's Leap* (page 18) where I used deep browns, burgundy and purple. You'll have more richly colored quilts if you design them using value, not just color.

If you're planning on augmenting your scraps with new fabrics, be sure to look for variegated prints and prints with long, horizontal bands of color. These are invaluable in landscape construction. Look carefully at the quilts *Foggy Fall* (page 86) and *Foggy Spring* (page 82). The main background fabric in both is a variegated batik ranging in value from medium to light. It does most of the work in creating the foggy illusion in the foreground and the gradual lightening in the tree canopy area.

Variegated prints will also help you create skies, water, sunsets and other scenic elements in which you need to create a value change. I usually buy ½ yard (.5m) pieces of these fabrics because they are so versatile.

The other type of print I find extremely helpful is one that looks hand-painted with different values and colors in horizontal patterns across the width of the print.

A value-finder tool can be very helpful when you are designing your landscape and choosing strips.

The variegated batik used for the background (indicated with arrows) is the backbone of the quilt top; other background strips were brought in to blend with it.

The style of strip-pieced landscape quilts allows you to blend pictorial realism with a contemporary artistic flair.

Blending solids and prints is not something I generally recommend unless the solid fabric is used as a "highlighting" strip. Notice the bright purple strips running through *Spring Branches* (page 108).

I routinely use skinny strips to add accent color and a bit of drama to the landscape. Use solid colors only in this capacity, or they may detract from the rest of your quilt by standing out like a sore thumb—unless you are creating a quilt of mostly solid-colored strips.

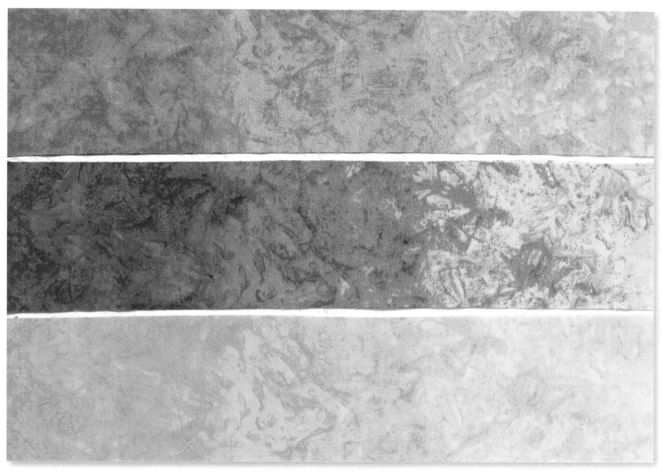

The prints shown here are excellent options because they have built-in value changes that will help you blend your fabrics. They can be the backbone of many elements you create, from deepening sunsets to water and skies.

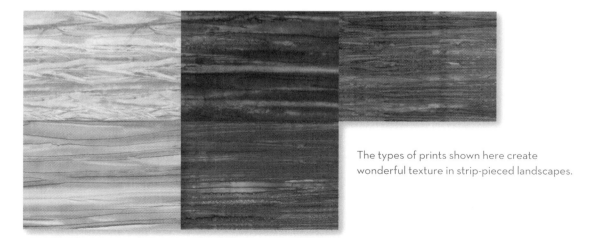

The types of prints shown here create wonderful texture in strip-pieced landscapes.

Design Considerations

Focal Points

In general, when designing an original landscape quilt, there are two things to keep in mind.

First, your landscape will need a focal point—something interesting to attract the viewer. Most of the time, this focal point will be the area in the quilt with the most value contrast, or it will be one of the objects you create in your quilt.

The most important thing to keep in mind regarding a focal point is where to put it—or should I say, where *not* to put it. Do not put the focal point in the center of the quilt; focal points are better placed off center, either vertically or horizontally, or both.

The other thing to keep in mind is that, in general, the darkest values will be used in the foreground. If you can design your landscape with this in mind, you will create depth and add space and dimension to your piece. The exceptions to this rule occur when creating an ocean or large body of water. When creating water, you might mix lighter strips in the darker foreground water to represent sunlight reflecting off the surface. Similarly, you may mix lighter fabrics in the foreground if you are creating a backlit landscape like *Blue Ridge Mountain Sunset* (page 116).

The focal point is easy to see in *Birches and Virginia Creeper* (page 100). It's the bright white tree trunks and dramatic dark branches.

Can you find the focal point in *The Watchman* (page 36)? (Hint: It is where the broken tree branches reach into the sky.)

The focal point is the sailboat in the project *Sailing* (page 78).

Construction Methods

Before you jump right in and begin cutting strips, you need to consider one other aspect of this type of quilt making: the method of landscape construction. Do you want to piece your strips? Fuse them? Glue them to a foundation? There are a few things to think about before you make this decision.

DESIGNING FOR STRIP-PIECED QUILTS

If you decide you would like to strip piece a landscape quilt, there are three things to keep in mind. The first is that you will need to cut your strips ½" (1.3cm) wider than the finished strip sizes to take into account the seam allowance when the strips are sewn together. The second thing to keep in mind is that, when arranging the strips on your design wall, you'll need to overlap them by ½" (1.3cm) so you can see your design taking shape. Lastly, are you picturing long, straight strips in your design—longer than say 30" (76.2cm)? If yes, I recommend piecing your strips.

When creating landscapes out of long, straight strips, I find it much easier to piece using a tear-away foundation, especially if I plan to include skinny, ¼"-wide (6mm) finished strips. Using a tear-away foundation means that you should cut your strips approximately ⅛" (3mm) shy of where you would normally cut them. For example, if you are constructing a landscape with a 1" (2.5cm) finished strip, you would normally cut your strips 1½" (3.8cm) wide. However, using a tear-away foundation requires that you cut them 1⅜" (3.5cm). The reason for this will become apparent in chapter 4, and I strongly recommend piecing using this method. Not only is it faster and easier, it is also more accurate and will keep the rows straight. You can see how important maintaining straight rows is in the example of *Lone Cypress Tree* (page 120).

When creating landscapes that are wider than about 20" (50.8cm), the danger in using a fusible or muslin foundation instead of a tear-away foundation is that straight rows will be hard to achieve. If you glue or fuse extremely long strips to a muslin background or fusible interfacing, keeping long strips perfectly horizontal or vertical can be tricky. You'll need to use a carpenter's corner square or T-square to measure from bottom to top or left to right after each strip to maintain straight strips. These foundations are also stretchy, so they will not necessarily keep straight

rows straight. On the other hand, if your quilt will only be approximately 20" (50.8cm) wide, using a fusible foundation to hold your strips and keep them straight is easy.

Of course, if you would like to piece long strips and don't really care if all your rows are perfectly straight, piece away! Then just trim the finished quilt top before you add borders. If the rows are a bit curved, it becomes part of the landscape's style.

DESIGNING FOR FUSED OR GLUED STRIP QUILTS

If you are going to create a landscape using strips and are not going to piece them, you will have a much easier time arranging your scene. You end up with what you see when you design; you don't see a change like when you piece strips, watching each shrink by ½" (1.3cm) per strip width. You don't have to take into account a seam allowance, which can make things like lining up hill slopes tricky.

On the other hand, you will have loose threads and raw edges with this method. Sometimes I really don't want to see loose threads, so I hide them by thread painting over the edges. This is just personal preference; you may not mind loose threads at all. Fusing and gluing strips to a foundation is faster and easier, especially in smaller projects. Creating a landscape with this method is much more spontaneous and fun.

These are some general thoughts and ideas to help you figure out what you would like to create and where to start. Now, let's get down to specifics.

Making a Graph Paper Map

Whether you piece your quilt or decide to fuse or glue strips of fabric to a foundation, mapping out your design on graph paper is very helpful. Assign a measurement to each square on the graph paper (for example 2" [5.1cm]). This doesn't mean your strips will be 2" (5.1cm) wide; it means you will need a certain length or width of strips to create 2" (5.1cm) of space in your quilt top. This is very important, because it lets you know when you should introduce another color or begin to create a feature in your landscape. For example, in my quilt *Lone Cypress Tree* (page 120), I needed to create a rocky bluff approximately 11" (27.9cm) high and 20" (50.8cm) long in a quilt measuring 41" × 32" (104.1cm × 81.3cm) in dimension. The number of strips I used to create the bluff didn't matter.

In *Sunset on the Lake* (page 48), I needed 5" (12.7cm) of foreground green before introducing water. Mapping out the design ahead of time makes arranging the strips much easier.

Look at my pattern for *The Watchman*, shown here. To create the distant bluff, I was very precise in selecting the strip lengths. Graph paper enabled me to do this. Each square equaled 2" (5.1cm), and my graph paper design actually became a pattern I could sew using a tear-away foundation. I filled up the 2" (5.1cm) spaces with strips which finished at 1¼" (3.2cm), ½" (1.3cm) and ¼" (6mm).

Your graph paper map will also help you decide the angle to sew strip sections together. For example, 45° angles produce a steeper slope than 30° angles. Using angles to build "steepness" will be covered in the next chapter. We'll also cover when not to vary the angles.

None of my projects use the same strip width throughout. You will create a much more satisfying landscape if you vary the width of your strips.

Working out your design on graph paper helps you arrange your strips.

These graph paper maps can be very precise.

27

Creating WITH STRIPS!

Make specific landscape features from fabric strips

It might seem a bit surprising how versatile straight strips of fabrics can be when creating landscapes. From Karen Tunnell's use of short, straight strips to create rocks and boulders (pages 12 and 13) to my use of long, straight, colorful strips to create sunsets and sweeping vistas, combining strips of different prints and textures is a dynamic and relatively simple way to create a picture.

In this chapter, I'll explain how to use strips to create various scenic elements, like skies, trees and water, in your landscapes.

MONUMENT VALLEY

78" × 41" (198.1cm × 10.4cm)
This landscape was inspired by a photograph of the Mittens Monument at sunset. I created my quilt in a triptych form to capture the broad, open, sweeping nature of the landscape.

Laying Out the Design

Pieced Landscapes

When laying out a pieced landscape, it is helpful to have a design wall to help hold the strips in place. A design wall can be built by pinning batting to a foam insulation panel. I find it easier to arrange the strips starting at the bottom and working up, but you can work in whichever way you are comfortable. During this process, finger press the angles you wish to create and pin them in place to your design wall. Angles, as you'll see in this chapter, are critical to achieving the desired effect when creating scenic elements.

I do not generally piece any strip segments (multiple fabrics along one strip) until my design is done. However, this isn't a hard-and-fast rule. When designing a more complicated landscape where mountain slopes or hills need to be closely aligned, it is easier to sew them together later or glue them in place on a foundation. Simple strip segments in which angles do not need to be closely aligned can be pieced during the design process.

Try to leave excess fabric dangling—do not cut strips short until you are very sure. I cut off excess only when I'm sewing everything together after the design is completed.

As you design, put a bit of masking tape on the portion of the strip signifying either the left or right side of the quilt top. Or, if you are creating a vertically oriented quilt, like *Wyoming Sunrise* (page 112) or one of the *Foggy* quilts (pages 82 and 84), place the tape marker at the top or the bottom of your strips. This will help you create the major landscape forms in your design. I learned this lesson the hard way! After creating the arched bluff for *Lover's Leap* (page 18) on my design wall, I tried to transfer the strips to a tear-away foundation, but I did not have a "reference point" marking the beginning and ending of each strip segment. As a result, when I moved each completed or sewn strip set, the whole arched bluff slid out of formation on the foundation and had to be redone. The bits of masking tape you add to the ends of each strip set will serve as reference points. (If you cut these ends off instead of using tape, you might run into trouble as you begin piecing your strip sets together; you could discover that you need an extra inch or two, and if you cut them, you won't have that extra amount.)

Non-Pieced Landscapes

If you are creating a non-pieced landscape, simply arrange your strips directly on the foundation, cutting and trimming as you create. You'll learn more about this method in the next chapter.

Lastly, don't forget to vary the sizes of your strip widths! I've seen many strip-pieced landscapes that would have been more successful if the quilter had varied the strip widths throughout the quilt. The easiest way to accomplish this is to set up a repetitive pattern of strip widths. This creates a nice rhythm and makes designing and constructing the quilt easier. You'll see how I use this rhythm of repeating strip widths throughout the projects. Generally speaking, my finished strips are rarely wider than 1¾" (4.4cm) and no narrower than ¼" (6mm). I rarely place two strips of the same width in adjacent positions.

Creating Angles

Whatever scenic element you are creating as you design and piece your landscape, the angle at which you adjoin two different strips of fabric is important. You will get different results when you sew two strips together using a 45° angle versus a more gradual 20° angle. You won't need to measure these angles in any precise way—no protractor necessary! You can simply estimate the angle by varying the direction you lay the top strip. Straight up and perpendicular to the bottom strip creates a 45° angle and produces a steep slope; if you gradually tilt that top strip to the left, the slope levels out.

This is important for creating steep mountain hillsides and flowing seas and skies. In areas where you need to build height in a mountain or hill using three or four strips, you will need to use 45° angles. If your design calls for eight to ten strips to create a hill or bluff, you can vary the angles to produce a more interesting and realistic slope, adding steepness to it in some places and leveling out others.

I almost always recommend using long 20° to 35° angles when combining strip segments to create sky and water. Long, gentle angles soften and blend the strips and look more natural; they lend themselves to flowing water and skies.

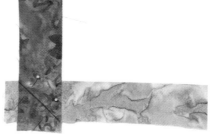

Two strips pinned to create a 45° angle. (The sewing line is drawn in pencil for reference.)

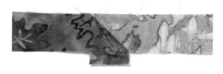

Sewn strips open in a 45° angle—a steep slope.

Two strips pinned to create a 35° angle. (The sewing line is drawn in pencil for reference.)

Sewn strips open in a 35° angle—a moderate slope.

Two strips pinned to create a 20° angle. (The sewing line is drawn in pencil for reference.)

Sewn strips open in a 20° angle—a gentle slope.

Mix up angles to create variety in your hill or mountain slopes.

Some of my skies combine batiks with blue sky landscape prints. Some use a different fabric every strip, and some use the same fabric for a few strips in a row. Generally speaking, skies are easiest to make when you keep lighter-value prints at the horizon line and gradually darken the values as you go higher into the sky. (Refer to *The Watchman* on page 36.) If you are designing using skinny highlighting strips, you can introduce deeper values with them or use them to introduce new colors. In *Monument Valley* (page 28), you'll see how I used narrow strips to introduce color and value changes.

When creating skies, use longer, narrower angles (20°–30°) to join strip segments. The longer angles look more flowing and gentler than the steeper 45° angles. (Binding strips are made using 45° angles.) It's also helpful to use uniform angles when creating a sky. If you use a 45° angle on one strip and a 20° angle on another, it can be jarring and may detract from the general smoothness you are trying to build into the sky.

Creating a sunset or sunrise can be a bit more challenging. Though you will want to use your boldest, most intense golden yellows, your sky will glow more if you use them sparingly. Use bold, intense, pure color with the following rule in mind: Less is more. (Or less is better!) Luminous sunsets and sunrises are created by using just a bit of rich color alongside fabrics that are whiter or lighter in value.

You can use narrow strips to introduce color and value changes.

The same fabric can be used in adjacent strips.

Skies Tip

One important thing to know about sky fabrics is that if you use a print with horizontal cloud formations and create your sky using vertical strips, your sky will look like blue-and-white zebra stripes. Be sure to consider the directionality of any prints, like cloud prints, prior to cutting to avoid problems like this.

Too much bold color will overwhelm the rest of the landscape, so use it sparingly. Arrows in the closeups indicate where I used the boldest strips of *Monument Valley* (top) and *Blue Ridge Mountain* (bottom).

Forests

The brighter green and purple strips break up the all-over foliage prints. They keep the landscape behind the saplings from being too dark and monotonous.

Creating background forests is as simple as using all-over tree landscape prints. Mix these fabrics together, add a few narrow strips of color, and your scene is ready for appliqué. I routinely mix brighter batik prints in with the all-over tree prints to add extra color and texture to my landscape. When creating a vertical forest, I use narrow strips of color to "highlight" the trees, to break up the solid-looking background and to add color and interest.

Meadows

Meadows are easy to construct. Just place strips with the darkest values in the foreground and combine a variety of green prints and even small floral prints. Meadows can be left plain, such as the meadow in *Sailing* (page 78), or they can be used as a background for appliqué.

Close-up of the meadow from *Strip-Pieced Spring* (page 68).

Water

Do you have blue fabric? If so, you have water. It's that simple. I primarily use smooth fabrics with long, horizontal striations in the print, as well as fabrics with tiny flowers. It's important to keep strips with similar texture together as you design. For example, I used tiny floral fabrics in *Sailing* (page 78) and long, flowing prints in *Lone Cypress Tree* (page 120). Remember not to mix smooth, solid-looking, tone-on-tone prints with busier prints when you're designing.

In most cases, the easiest way to create a sunlit water surface is to combine narrow "highlighting" strips of light blues or white fabrics with deeper-value blue fabrics. You can also bring in violets when you create water.

When piecing water, use longer, narrower angles (20°–30°) to sew together strip segments. Your water prints will blend together more easily when you use longer angles to sew your strip segments together.

Water doesn't always need to be blue. In art quilts you are free to bring in all kinds of color. In *Wildflowers by the Sea* (page 74), I added pink and lavender.

Hills and Mountains

Creating hills and mountains can be as simple as joining two strips of fabric—one strip of mountain fabric and one strip of background fabric. You can sew the two strips together creating the same 45° angle used to join binding strips, or you can use other angles to create sloping hills or steep mountains.

These bluffs in *Strip-Pieced Spring* (page 68) are mainly created using 45° angles.

Mix the angles to create a natural-looking rock outcropping, as shown here in *Lone Cypress Tree* (page 120).

Mix the angles to create sweeping vertical rises and gently falling slopes, as shown here in *Wyoming Sunrise* (page 112).

Construction
OF
STRiPS!

*Piecing and non-piecing methods
for quilt top construction*

If you choose to piece your strip quilt, you will need to cut your strips and sew them with perfect seam allowances. You will need to sew your angles together perfectly as well. To achieve this level of precision, it is very helpful to starch and press the fabric before cutting strips. After you sew two strip segments together, press them together as sewn to set the seam, and then open the strips and press the seam allowance toward the darker strip. From cutting to sewing, precision piecing is essential. Do this for every stitched seam. If you are aiming for perfectly straight rows, you still might have problems.

It is time for true confessions: I hate precision piecing. I find it tedious and frustrating. I found a better way. Let's all do the happy dance!

THE WATCHMAN

49" × 41" (124.5cm × 104.1cm)
Using graph paper, I was able to design and create the distant mountains using vertical strips, and fit them into a landscape predominately created with horizontal strips.

Using a Tear-Away Foundation

Oftentimes, even though we are very accurate in strip piecing, we end up with curved seams. This is because the weights and weaves of our various fabrics pull differently. Some of them stretch out more than others; some have a looser weave and are "wimpier" fabrics. This is why I rarely sew one strip to another in the traditional way. I use a tear-away foundation to piece. My preferred product is Create-A-Pattern by Bosal; it comes on a bolt and is 46" (116.8cm) wide.

This method is very fast, and the extra support from the foundation keeps even my narrow ¼"-wide (6mm) finished rows straight and even. I have even used this method with stretchy corduroy fabric; the tear-away foundation generated enough support to keep my straight rows straight.

While designing your quilt, you placed pins and left strips hanging everywhere. Now is the time to get the strip segments sewn together, trimmed and organized. We will do this by creating a foundation out of tear-away stabilizer. We will draw rows with a pen, glue our strips to the rows, fold along the rows and stitch ¼" (6mm) from the edge of the folds. It's not as complicated as it sounds! It's actually easier and more forgiving, and it will go a long way toward keeping your straight rows straight. (Quilt show judges love that!) If your pieced angles aren't quite perfect, no problem. If you have cut your strips less than perfectly, no problem. Using a tear-away foundation hides all of those imperfections!

Let's take this one step at a time.

1 Draft plumb lines: These will be the finished outside edges of two sides of your landscape. Cut off the required amount of tear-away foundation (provided in the project instructions). If the foundation is wrinkled, use a cool iron to press it. Tape the foundation to a large rotary cutting mat so it overlaps the mat's 1" (2.5cm) measuring lines, both horizontally and vertically. You will be able to see the mat's 1" (2.5cm) line through the foundation. Use a ballpoint pen to draw 2 perpendicular 1" (2.5cm) lines on your foundation (Figure 1). These are your plumb lines; they are two fixed reference points that you will need when arranging and sewing together the strips.

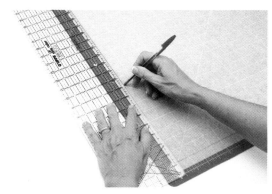

Figure 1: Draw plumb lines.

2 Draft fold-and-sew lines: Use a ballpoint pen and draw along the measuring lines of the rotary cutting mat. If your foundation is not thin enough for this, you can use your rotary ruler to draw the lines. If you are creating one of the projects in this book, the directions will tell you on which widths to draw your fold-and-sew lines. In my example here, the finished strip widths will be 1" (2.5cm), ¾" (1.9cm) and ¼" (6mm) in repeating order. This means I will draft fold-and-sew lines of 1½" (3.8cm), 1¼" (3.2cm) and ¾" (1.9cm) all the way along this piece of foundation (Figure 2). You will be gluing fabric strips between these fold-and-sew lines, folding the foundation along each line and stitching ¼" (6mm) from the edge of each of them. After the lines are drawn, set the foundation aside.

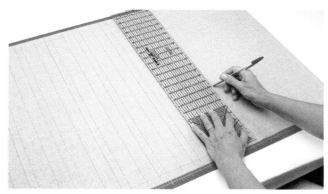

Figure 2: Draw fold-and-sew lines on the foundation.

3 Sew the strip segments together: Your landscape is made of multiple strips of fabric, and some of those strips are made by piecing together two or more fabrics. The first thing to do is piece those strip segments together.

Carefully unpin one strip segment from your design board, keeping track of where the true quilt top edge will start. (There should be a piece of masking tape there.) Use an iron and press the angle you wish to create on the strip (Figure 3). Then open the strip and sew along the crease, pinning as necessary (Figure 4). Press the seam and trim off the excess (Figures 5 and 6). Do this for all the simple strip segments. Place the finished strips back in place on the design wall.

If you have complicated strip segments with three or more strips to connect, or if you need the finished strips and their angles to align properly when the quilt top is sewn together (for example, if you are creating a smooth hill slope or mountain and need seams to match) do not sew these strips together. Simply keep them pinned in place for now, and don't trim off any fabric you consider excess.

Figure 3: Press the pinned strips.

Figure 5: Press the seam allowance toward the darker fabric.

Figure 4: Sew along the crease.

Figure 6: Trim off the excess fabric. It is not necessary to trim to an exact ¼" (6mm), but do maintain a seam allowance.

4 Glue your strips to the foundation: Transfer your completed strip sets to the foundation one at a time using a paper glue stick (Figure 7). (It is not necessary to buy a fabric glue stick; a simple water-soluble glue stick will work, but don't use the kind that turns blue when wet.) Swipe the glue stick on your foundation down the center of two drawn lines; try to keep the glue 1/4" (6mm) away from the seam allowances. (I usually start at the bottom of the design and work my way up, or at the top and work my way down.)

To transfer complicated strips segments, use a glue stick to create the finished angle in the top strip and then to secure it in the right place over the bottom strip. This is a much simpler way of aligning strip angles to create a smooth slope. Begin by pressing the angle into the top strip. Open the strip and swipe the crease with the glue stick (Figure 8), then trim off any excess fabric (Figure 9). In this example, I am creating a dark foreground slope over a distant meadow.

Now, take the top strip with the glued angle and arrange it over the bottom strip. Glue the top strip in place. When I created the distant green hill in my next example (Figure 10), I glued down the peach and blue sky fabric strips first. I then arranged the green hill strips over them, taking into account the 1/4" (6mm) seam allowances so my hillside would line up nicely when I folded and sewed along my draft lines.

The easiest way to arrange these types of hillside slopes is to mark 1/4" (6mm) from the edge of the strip where the hill meets the sky using a wash-out marker.

In Figure 10, you can see those blue dots of the washout marker and how I arranged the hill strips over the sky strips. When I sew these rows, the blue dots will align, assuring me that the hillside angles will align.

After the top strips are glued in place, pin them down and trim off the excess fabric from the bottom strip (Figure 11).

Most of the projects in this book do not require this meticulous piecing, but I wanted to show you how it can be done in case you want to align adjacent strips to keep slope angles close together.

Figure 7: Smooth on a fabric strip.

Figure 8: Swipe the crease with the glue stick and pinch it shut.

Figure 9: Cut off the excess fabric. It is not necessary to leave a precise 1/4" (6mm) seam allowance.

Figure 10: Line up the two marks so that when the ¼" (6mm) seam is sewn, the angles will meet.

Figure 11: Glue down the angles and trim off the excess fabric underneath.

5 Stitch down the glued angles: If your design has portions where angles are merely glued down and not sewn, you will need to sew them in place; use a straight stitch along the folded edge. I recommend monofilament thread so the stitching won't be noticeable, but you can use a matching thread if you like (Figure 12).

6 Fold and sew: Carefully fold the foundation along the lines you drew, right sides together, and sew ¼" (6mm) from the edge of each fold. Use a large needle (at least a 90/14, preferably a 100/16) and use tiny stitches. This will create tiny perforations along the seam line, which will help you to tear away the foundation more easily. As you fold and sew, make sure the fabric strips are not bunched up along the seam allowances. (This is why I recommended that you cut your strips ⅛" [3mm] thinner than you drew on your foundation.) Pin the foundation closed as you fold and sew each row to help keep the strips from folding over on the edges (Figure 13).

Occasionally your design will include finished ¼" (6mm) highlighting strips. Even using a tear-away foundation, these long, straight, very skinny strips can be difficult to sew. For these fold and sew rows, use your ¼" (6mm) presser foot but align the *left* side of the foot with the previously sewn seam. The foot will snug up against the ridge of the seam from the other side, and you'll be able to sew a perfect finished row (Figures 14a and 14b).

Figure 12: Stitch down your glued strip angles.

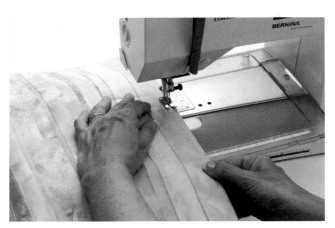

Figure 13: Fold and sew along the grid lines. Use a large needle and tiny stitches.

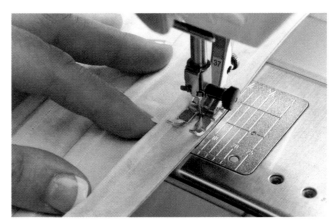

Figure 14a: Use the left side of your presser foot to align the seam.

7 Tear away the foundation: Tear the foundation away from the seam allowances. Don't worry about getting every little bit—the foundation is light and will not affect the way the fabric hangs when it is quilted (Figure 15).

8 Press the strips: Before pressing the quilt top, be sure to remove any markings you might have made when arranging your strips (for example, the ¼" [6mm] alignment marks). Working from the back of the quilt top, press the strips in one direction or another, pressing toward the darkest strips when possible (Figure 16). It is easiest to press the narrow ¼" (6mm) strips with both seam allowances going away from the strip. Use an iron on medium heat with no steam; the foundation and the glue will burn easily if overheated. When this is done, press the quilt top from the front using an iron on medium heat with a little steam.

9 Add appliqué: If your project includes appliqué or embroidery, now is the time to add it. The remaining foundation on the back of the quilt top will add stability and keep the rows straight during the fusing process.

10 Trim the edges: Turn your foundation to the back and trim along the drawn plumb lines. Add borders if desired.

11 Tear off the remaining foundation: Remove the remaining foundation, but don't tug and pull. If it doesn't come off easily, leave it. You can quilt right through it without a problem. If you are making a large wall hanging, though, the added weight of the quilt top with the foundation still intact makes it a little more difficult to maneuver during the quilting process, so remove as much of the foundation as possible.

12 Add borders and baste: Add borders if desired and baste your quilt top to your batting only. Do not add backing.

Figure 14b: Perfect ¼" (6mm) seams.

Figure 15: Tear away the foundation from the seam allowances.

Figure 16: Press the seams flat.

Using a Fusible Interfacing

If all of this has you trembling in fear, there is another way to create a landscape using strips. You can simply use a glue stick and glue your strips to a lightweight muslin foundation. Or you can use a fusible tricot interfacing as your foundation, which is my preferred method. It is so easy! Just cut your strips and assemble. There is no seam allowance to take into account, so designing is a snap. What you see is what you get. Just arrange your strips, cut out your angles and use your glue stick to attach them to the background strip. Then fuse it all in place to the foundation.

When purchasing a foundation for this purpose, avoid the kind with the little dots of glue. Look for a lightweight tricot knit with a fusible web on one side. (This is a widely available product at sewing stores.) Place the product rough-side up on a table and arrange fabrics on top of it. When I am satisfied with my design, I simply press with an iron. If I'm following a pattern (for example, *A Pastoral* on page 88), I lay a life-size pattern beneath the foundation so I can see it through the foundation and simply arrange the fabrics on top according to the pattern.

Pressing Tip

Be careful of your table top! Steam and high heat might warp the finish. I use an old card table or a piece of plywood with a towel. You can also anchor your finished design carefully and then carry the foundation to an ironing board to fuse the design in place.

1 Arrange the strips: To create a landscape with perfectly horizontal and even strips, lay your fusible foundation rough-side up on a table or board. Build the design starting at the bottom of the interfacing by arranging strips and measuring the distance from the bottom after each strip is in place (Figure 1). (Or conversely, start at the top of the foundation and work your way down, measuring after each strip.) Glue and trim any angles as you design.

As you arrange the strips, it is very helpful to have a warm iron on hand to lightly press the strips in place without fully activating the glue. I usually work two to three rows at a time before lightly pressing with a warm (not hot) iron. If you choose not to do this, don't sneeze or bump the table, or all those carefully arranged rows could be compromised.

2 Fuse the strips in place: After the design is in place, follow the manufacturer's directions for your fusible product and fuse the strips in place (Figure 2).

3 Add borders and baste: Add borders if desired and baste your quilt top to your batting only. Do not add backing.

4 Sew the edges: Landscapes made with fused or glued strips of fabrics will need to be stitched at the edges to hold them in place during the quilting process. When you quilt, unquilted portions of the quilt top become puffier than quilted portions, which is a natural part of the process. When strips are not stitched down, they can warp and pull out of place. As I mentioned earlier, sometimes thready raw edges bother me. To solve both issues, I recommend setting your sewing machine to a wide zigzag and use monofilament to stitch down the edges. Do this before you add your backing. (More about this process can be found in chapter 6.)

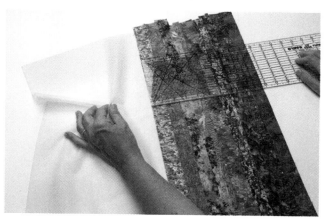

Figure 1: Measure carefully from the bottom to the top to keep horizontal rows straight and even.

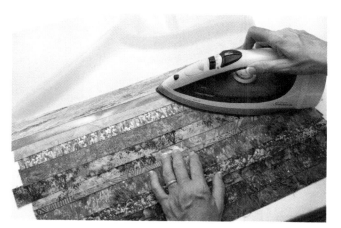

Figure 2: Fuse in place.

String Piecing

If you have lots of scraps in all shapes and sizes, then boy, do I have a method for you. I absolutely love string piecing. I can throw on my favorite movie and sew, sew, sew without having to think too hard. Start by organizing your scraps and gathering strips of fabric. I sew with my large scissors handy and just cut strips from leftover remnants as needed. No particular sizes or widths are required. You can use 2"–3" (5.1cm–7.6cm) wide strips or narrow ¾" (1.9cm) wide strips, and mix in the little strings you have in your pile of scraps. Let's get started!

String Piecing Tip

String piecing can be done on a tear-away foundation or on lightweight muslin. Any size block can be created with strings, and they can be pieced vertically or diagonally. Wonky log cabin blocks are also easily created with strings. String piecing is a terrific way to use up scraps and remnants!

1 Cut out the foundation segments: Cut out squares of tear-away foundation. For this example, I used 5" (12.7cm) squares and pieced them on a diagonal. Swipe your glue stick corner to corner down the center and lay out a strip of fabric (Figure 1).

2 Sew the strips together: Arrange a second strip right sides together with the first and sew down one aligned edge (Figure 2). Use tiny stitches and a large needle. It is not necessary to sew perfectly parallel strips—they can be angled and wedge shaped.

3 Press: Open up the strips and press in place. Then use a glue stick to anchor the second strip to the foundation (Figure 3).

4 Continue adding strips: Repeat the previous steps until the foundation block is full (Figure 4). Create as many blocks as the pattern requires.

5 Finish the blocks: Tear away the foundation. Spray with starch and press each block using steam. Trim each block to a uniform size.

6 Assemble the quilt top: Sew the blocks together to create the quilt top.

Figure 2: Sew ¼" (6mm) from the edge of the strips.

Figure 3: Anchor the second strip in place with glue.

Figure 1: Glue your first fabric strip to the foundation.

Figure 4: Fill the foundation with strips.

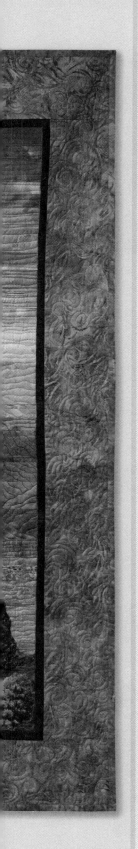

Embellishing YOUR STRiPS!

Spice up your landscape with embellishments and appliqué

Sometimes a landscape quilt is ready to be quilted once the strips are assembled or pieced. Other times, however, you may first want to add all kinds of fun stuff to your quilt top. I consider many of my strip-pieced landscapes as backdrops for the main event. The *Foggy* quilts (pages 82 and 86), for example, only work because of the appliquéed leaves and flowers. *Blue Ridge Mountain Sunset* (page 116) would feel empty without the blooming azaleas in the foreground that pick up the sunset colors. In this chapter, I'll show you a few things you can do to add interest, texture and beauty to your quilt top.

SUNSET ON THE LAKE

48" × 41" (121.9cm × 104.1cm)
I decided to add the red tulle highlights to the water after the quilt was finished. They were easy to create and made a big difference in the quilt.

Broderie Perse Appliqué

Broderie perse appliqué is far and away the fastest and easiest way to add interest to your landscape. If you can find the perfect flowers and leaves, all you have to do is cut them out and glue or fuse them to your landscape. For this type of appliqué, I prefer to use Steam-A-Seam. Following the manufacturer's instructions, I lightly press the fusible product to the wrong side of the flower or leaf fabric and cut out exactly the shape I need. After the paper backing is removed, the fusible web is lightly sticky and allows me to try out various placements on my quilt top before fusing it in place.

In this quilt, mountain azaleas were created by cutting out clumps of flowers and leaves.

Creating Shrubbery

I often make collages on top of a fusible web to create bushes and thick evergreen trees. To do this, create a pattern for the shape of the desired tree or bush by drawing it on paper and cutting it out. Draw the pattern in reverse on the paper side of your choice of paper-backed fusible web (I use both Wonder-Under and Steam-A-Seam). Fuse an all-over tree or shrubbery fabric to this shape and cut it out (Figure 1).

Next, messy cut clumps from another all-over print to add different highlights and texture on top (Figure 2). Use a glue stick to anchor these patches. They will be sewn down later as part of the quilting process. (See chapter 6.)

Figure 1: Create a base tree from the darker print.

Figure 2: Use a glue stick to add lighter patches to one side of the tree.

Adding Shading and Highlights

Adding shading to tree trunks and branches with a fabric dye marker is quite easy. Use brown, black or gray markers to create deep shadows, or use a white marker to add pale highlights. Bright yellow markers give a sun-kissed effect to flowers and leaves. It is best to use the markers before you fuse on your appliqué because the lumpy seams of your patchwork underneath will be hard to work around after the appliqué is fused in place. You can see how highlighting and shading created natural-looking branches in *Strip Pieced Spring* (page 68) and *Strip Pieced Fall* (page 72).

Shading is especially helpful in creating three-dimensional effects. The tree trunks in *Birches and Virginia Creeper* (page 100) look round and solid because they are shaded on one side.

Assorted fabric dye markers make highlighting and shading a snap.

Highlighting with a silver metallic marker gives a more ornamental sun-kissed effect.

Creating a Collage

Another easy way to add texture or create fine tree leaves is to use a product called Sulky Super Solvy to create a collage. (Sulky Super Solvy is widely available at craft stores.) This product feels like a thick plastic wrap, but it is not plastic and dissolves in water. Let's look at one way to use this marvelous product.

1 Prepare: Cut out two pieces of Super Solvy (Figure 1).

2 Add tulle: Add a layer of tulle, choosing a color most resembling the background of your quilt top (Figure 2). In this example, I used white tulle because I'm creating a tree canopy with a light yellow and light blue background.

3 Sprinkle on bits of fabric: Because I'm creating a tree canopy, I'm sprinkling on snippets of medium and dark green fabrics, as well as some light blue bits. My snippets are no larger than ¼" (6mm) (Figure 3).

4 Layer and press: Layer the second piece of Super Solvy on top of the fabric collage and press according to the manufacturer's directions (Figure 4). I use a fiberglass pressing sheet made by Bo-Nash to protect the fragile tulle.

Figure 2: Super Solvy with tulle.

Figure 3: Create a collage of tiny snippets of fabric.

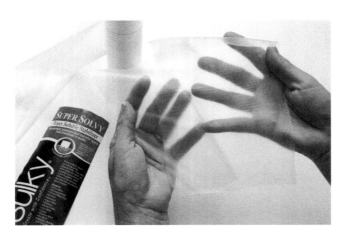

Figure 1: Cut two pieces of Super Solvy.

Figure 4: Press the Super Solvy layers together.

5 Sew: Stitch the layers together. The tiny snippets need a lot of dense stitching to hold them in place. Stitch over and around in tiny loops with a variegated thread (Figure 5).

6 Soak: Soak and resoak the collage in water as necessary to dissolve the Super Solvy product (Figure 6). Blot with absorbent towels and be patient.

7 Cut out portions of your collage: Cut out messy shapes or jigsaw puzzle shapes from the collage (Figure 7).
   The shapes can now be arranged on your quilt top. Use a glue stick, tiny bits of a fusible web or Bo-Nash Bonding Powder to temporarily anchor the small shapes in place. Stitch them down during the quilting process or after basting the quilt top to the batting (Figure 8). (See directions in chapter 6.)

Figure 6: Soak the Super Solvy collage in water.

Figure 7: Messy cut shapes.

Figure 5: Stitch through the collage using a dense stitching pattern.

Figure 8: The tree leaves in *A Pastoral* (page 88) utilize this technique.

Creating Shadow and Light

You can add shadows and highlights to your landscape by using tulle. Use one or more layers of tulle, depending on how dark you would like the shadows to be or how much you would like to highlight sunny areas. Add the tulle by pinning it in place and stitching around the edges. It can also be fused down using a powder called Bo-Nash 007 Bonding Agent (Figure 1), though this product will give the tulle a somewhat shiny appearance.

To use Bo-Nash powder, lightly dampen the area where you would like to place the appliqué or tulle, sprinkle on the powder and gently blow away the excess. Then add your appliqué or tulle and press using the fiberglass pressing sheet that comes in the powder kit.

An easy way to add multiple layers of tulle is to use the Bo-Nash powder to fuse the layers together. Simply add tulle, sprinkle with a bit of the powder and add another layer of tulle as desired (Figure 2).

Figure 1: 007 Bonding Agent by Bo-Nash is a fusible powder.

Figure 2: Multiple layers can be fused together, and shapes can be cut out as desired.

Tulle is used to create the sun beams in *Blue Ridge Mountain Sunset* (page 116).

In *Sunset on the Lake* (page 48), I fused two layers of red tulle to create sunset reflections in the water.

Quilting YOUR STRiPS!

Finish your landscape

After your quilt top is completed, the artistry doesn't have to end! But that doesn't mean that the quilting needs to be complicated and precise. Natural-looking landscape quilts don't necessarily lend themselves to ornate quilting patterns; in fact, the simple stipple is sometimes best. Before automatically adding a border, if that is your habit, try visualizing your quilt without it. Perhaps the landscape looks better without a frame. If you wish to add borders, I strongly recommend that you bring your landscape with you as you shop. Lay it out with different choices and find a color that enhances the quilt top but doesn't overpower it. Also, before you begin quilting, remember to stitch down any appliqués and consider adding some thread painting.

WYOMING SUNRISE
48½" × 51" (121.9cm × 104.1cm)
While working on this quilt, I was playing with narrow vertical highlighting strips and discovered they create lovely 3-dimensional effects.

Finishing the Quilt

Basting with a Fusible Web

I recommend using a fusible web to baste your quilts. Wonder-Under is my preference, but plenty of other choices are available. Wonder-Under is available on a bolt without the paper backing. Lay out long sections of the fusible web on top of your batting. (I prefer to use 100% cotton batting. The weight and thickness of the batt keeps wall quilts straight and smooth against the wall when hung.) Smooth the quilt top on top of the fusible web.

When placing the quilt top onto the fusible web and batting sandwich, use a corner square or a similar carpentry tool to make sure the quilt top has perfect 90° corners and that both sides, or the top and the bottom of the quilt, are the same dimensions. Pull and fudge in extra fabric as needed. If there are somewhat puffier areas, keep those places in mind and quilt more heavily in them.

Stitching the Appliqués

When you're finished arranging your quilt top, gently press using steam. Don't slide your iron! Just lift and place the iron on the quilt top. After the top and batting are fused, stitch down any raw edge strips or appliqués.

The best way to minimize loose threads when stitching down the long edges of strips is to use a wide zigzag stitch with monofilament thread. If you don't mind loose threads, you can use a straight stitch instead. (After you quilt over the top of those stitches, the monofilament will be virtually unseen.)

When you are stitching down appliqués, you can use a matching thread, an invisible monofilament thread or a contrasting thread to create a decorative edge.

During this part of the process, you can also add some thread painting. Look at the tree from *Lone Cypress Tree* (page 120). Some of the textured zigzag stitching was done before the backing was added to the quilt sandwich. I used a dark green thread to anchor the tree foliage to the quilt top. After the backing was added, I quilted it using the same zigzag motion with a lighter variegated thread.

The zigzag stitch along the strip edges is hardly noticeable when the quilting is done.

Thread-painted Indian paintbrush wildflowers add one more decorative touch to *Wyoming Sunrise* (page 112).

Some of the thread play was done before the backing was added in *Lone Cypress Tree* (page 120).

Adding the Backing

The backing doesn't need to be fused on as thoroughly as the quilt top. Just rip off small 1" (2.5cm) bits of fusible web and place them every 4" (10.2cm) across the back of your quilt. Then fuse the backing in place.

Quilting

Quilting these types of landscapes can be quite easy. Simple stipple or meander quilting adds texture and is often more appropriate to pictorial landscape quilts than intricate fans, feathers or geometric circular motifs. If you are just beginning, quilting long, wavy lines across your strips is not only simple but can be the best way to enhance the quilt top. You can use your machine's walking foot or a free-motion foot to quilt long, wavy rows. I prefer using variegated thread when I quilt because the colors add more texture, and the value changes in the thread add even more interest to the landscape.

QUILTING SKIES

There are many ways to quilt skies, but here are the four types of quilting I use most. The first is long, wavy horizontal lines. Sometimes these lines can get "bumpy" in places to suggest clouds. You can also outline areas in your sky prints if clouds are part of the print pattern.

The long, wavy horizontal can be stitched densely or sparsely. *Lone Cypress Tree* (shown here) was quilted more sparsely, while *Lover's Leap* (page 18) was stitched densely, adding tiny back-and-forth hooks as necessary.

The second way to quilt a sky is by using a meander stipple. This works well on soft, impressionistic sky fabrics.

The third way I routinely quilt skies is with a blend of quilting and thread painting. This is done using a long back-and-forth motion in variegated threads that do not necessarily match the sky fabric.

The fourth way to quilt a sky is by using a long, flowing horizontal V-shaped curve. In a variegated thread, this design looks natural and coordinates with the style of strip piecing itself.

Long, wavy quilting lines can get bumpy in places to suggest clouds, as shown here in *Lone Cypress Tree* (page 120).

If you use a meander stipple, it should be long and flowing as shown in *Strip-Pieced Fall* (top) and *Strip-Pieced Spring* (bottom)—not a tight jigsaw puzzle shape.

Thread painting can add color, interest and beauty to an otherwise plain sky, as shown here in *A Pastoral* (page 88).

Choose a variegated thread that blends with and highlights the various colors of your sky fabrics.

QUILTING WATER

The most effective way to quilt water is to quilt long, wavy horizontal lines. The size of the waves should get bigger as the water gets closer to the foreground. The waves should be smoother and straighter the closer they get to the horizon line. Variegated blue threads with lights and darks will add to the impression of sunlight on the water. It is fine to cross over previously stitched rows of quilting when quilting water, especially as you move toward the horizon line where denser stitching will add to the illusion of distance.

The farther away the water is, the straighter the line of stitching should be.

QUILTING HILLS AND MOUNTAINS

Hills and mountains can be stippled, or they can be quilted by creating jagged crevasses down the slopes. Begin by quilting a somewhat parallel line following the angles of your strips. Then break off from quilting even parallel lines and bunch some together more closely and some farther apart. This technique works with both vertical and horizontal strip-pieced mountains. (See the detail photograph from *Wyoming Sunrise* [page 112] for an example of quilting with mountains made of vertical strips.)

You can break up larger bluff shapes by creating crevasses and hills within a larger pieced mountain. Look at the deep shadowed hill in *Blue Ridge Mountain Sunset* (shown here). Texture and interest was added by quilting smaller hills and mounds within the single dark blue bluff.

Break up large hills by creating small hills within and echo quilting the smaller hill shapes, as in *Blue Ridge Mountain Sunset* (page 116).

This mountain range in *Sunset on the Lake* (page 48) was pieced with horizontal strips and quilted with a variety of echo stitching styles.

QUILTING THE FOREGROUND

I usually stipple the foreground and outline stitch any leaves or flowers that might be present. Once again, variegated thread catches light here and there and adds to the texture and interest of the landscape. Foreground prints are often busier, so more complicated stitching patterns simply will not show against them.

Simple stippling and quilting around the ferns is all that is needed to finish this quilt.

Adding tiny circles in variegated threads adds interest and mimics the leaves and flowers in the foreground, as shown here in *Blue Ridge Mountain Sunset* (page 116).

STIPPLING

In landscape quilting, stippling the entire quilt can sometimes be too much. However, this is not the case when quilting over busy prints because your stitches will simply not show up. This is especially true when quilting the string-pieced projects in this book. In those cases, just meander or stipple the entire quilt top.

Quilts such as *Foggy Fall* and *Foggy Spring* are meant to be more abstract. It would be very hard to quilt elements such as sky or hills because of the tiny, narrow highlighting strips brought into the design. In these cases, simply stipple the entire quilt, bringing in contrasting thread around the leaves and flowers.

In *Birches and Virginia Creeper* (page 100), the background of the trees and the vine is simply stippled. The leaves are outline stitched, and a white thread is used to create the veins.

In *Foggy Fall* (page 86), the background is stipple quilted with a lightly colored variegated thread. A dark thread is used to quilt the leaves and the surrounding area.

Quilting tiny loops, circles and flowers adds interest to appliquéed elements in your landscape, as shown here in *Foggy Spring* (page 82).

Blocking and Binding

After the quilting is done, block your quilt. If you are confident that none of your fabric will bleed, simply soak the quilt in cold water and spin out the excess. Stretch the quilt out in a clean, carpeted area, and use carpentry rulers to ensure 90° corners. Use pins to anchor the quilt in the carpet as you work, stretching and smoothing various areas as necessary. Let the quilt dry for twenty-four hours.

If you have used fabric in strong, deep colors (especially red), do not soak your quilt. In these cases, lay the quilt flat in a clean, carpeted area and lightly mist it with water. Use rulers and pins to ensure perfect corners. After your quilt top is pinned in place, use a steam iron and a pressing cloth to thoroughly steam the quilt. Then let it dry for twenty-four hours.

Once the quilt is completely dry, trim off the border edges and excess backing and batting, and bind your quilt. All my bindings are single fold and are made from 1¼" (3.2cm) strips (for a narrow binding) or 1½" (3.8cm) strips (for a slightly wider binding). Don't forget to add a sleeve so you can easily hang your quilt, and be sure to sign your name to the back.

Now that you have read all about creating these landscapes, let's get started on making them. There are lots of projects to try out. Feel free to vary the patterns and use them as stepping stones to create your own personalized landscapes.

THE Projects

Projects to get you started

The projects in this chapter are arranged in order from simple to more complex. The complexity is determined by the necessity of lining up strip angles, the use of long, narrow 20° angles and sewing narrow ¼" (6mm) strips. Feel free to adapt any project to your own wishes and to use the provided tissue paper patterns as you'd like. All your strips should be sewn using a ¼" (6mm) presser foot or a ¼" (6mm) seam allowance.

Because most of these projects will only require a strip or two of various fabrics, the best way to approach them is to gather your scraps and stashed fabrics and arrange each color group in order from light to dark. Carefully look at the project pictures, and if you have to buy fabrics to augment your stash, buy ⅛–¼ yard (.1m–.2m) pieces. Be sure to look at the wrong side of your fabrics—the right side may not fit the project, but the wrong side might be perfect!

I piece most of my strips using a tear-away foundation, so the project instructions will refer you to chapter 4 for construction techniques. Included in the project directions are diagrams with plumb line measurements and the layout used for a particular brand of foundation (Create-A-Pattern by Bosal). This foundation comes on a bolt and is 46" (116.8cm) wide, but it can be hard to find. You can substitute any other lightweight foundation (adjusting for product dimensions), or you can buy the Bosal product online through my store (www.cathygeier.com). See the Resources

(page 125) for a local distributor of the Bosal product. Feel free to strip piece the projects in the traditional way of sewing two strips together. Starch and press each row to help keep straight strips straight.

Yardage requirements for each project are rough estimates. As you gather your fabrics, try to think in terms of how many strips you will need rather than how many yards (meters) of fabric you will need.

When I use the words "strip set," I'm referring to one completed strip length that includes more than one fabric. (For example, a single strip that includes water and land fabrics, or land and sky, would be considered one strip set.)

Lastly, many of the projects have fabric placement guidelines designed to help you know when to introduce another landscape feature. These guides show you, for example, how many inches (centimeters) of foreground you need to create before introducing water. Or how many inches (centimeters) of water you need to fill with fabric strips before you introduce the horizon line, or how long the base of a mountain needs to be. These guidelines are given in finished measurements. This is because, as you create your picture on your design wall, you will be slightly overlapping each strip of fabric so you can tell how your design is progressing. These placement guidelines, coupled with the strip widths I've given you, will help create a similar landscape in your own fabrics. Understand that your quilt will look different than mine—but it will be just as nice or even better!

APPLE BLOSSOM TIME

27" × 28½" (121.9cm × 104.1cm)
A simple strip-pieced landscape is the perfect setting for a tree branch.

Strip-Pieced Spring

26½" × 36½" (67.3cm × 92.7cm)

This simple landscape uses a repeating pattern of three finished 1" (2.5cm) strips and one finished ½" (1.3cm) strip alternating the height of the quilt. The angles used to create the bluffs are mostly 45°, the same angle used to create long binding strips. The width of the quilt makes it fat quarter friendly.

Materials

22" × 46" (55.9cm × 116.8cm) lightweight, tear-away foundation

⅓ yard (.3m) foreground greens and meadow fabrics

⅓ yard (.3m) water fabrics

¼ yard (.2m) lighter green island fabrics

⅓ yard (.3m) sky fabrics

¼ yard (.2m) mixed flower fabrics

4" × 6" (10.2cm × 15.2cm) scrap of green fabric for the stems

Scrap of brown fabric to make the branches

¼ yard (.2m) green leaf fabrics

⅛ yard (.1m) inner border fabric

½ yard (.5m) outer border and binding fabric

Batting

1 yard (.9m) backing fabric

Supplies

1 yard (.9m) of 18"-wide (45.7cm) paper-backed fusible web for appliqué

2 yards (1.8m) of 18"-wide (45.7cm) fusible web for quilt basting

Glue stick

Freezer paper

White highlighting marker

Dark brown dye or fabric marker

Tissue patterns: Branch 1, Branch 2

46" (116.8cm)

22" (55.9cm)

Draw plumb lines on the foundation

Instructions

1 Press the foundation to remove any wrinkles and draft the plumb lines. Add the fold-and-sew lines running parallel to the short 22" (55.9cm) side of the foundation. Starting at the bottom of the foundation, draw a repeating pattern of three 1½"-wide (3.8cm) strips and then one 1"-wide (2.5cm) strip. Repeat this pattern, filling the foundation and ending at the top with a 1½" (3.8cm) strip.

2 Cut the strips of fabric. Remember to cut the strips ⅛" (3mm) narrower than the fold-and-sew lines if you are using a tear-away foundation to piece. For this quilt, cut the strips 1⅜" (3.5cm) and ⅞" (2.2cm) wide.

3 Arrange the strips on a design wall, slightly overlapping them by ½" (1.3cm) so you can better visualize how the project will look when completed. As you design, remember to place a bit of tape on the end of each strip to signify the outermost edge of the quilt. Finger press angles in the lighter green strips to form the small islands and pin them over the edges of the water fabric strips.

4 When you are satisfied with the design, refer to the construction steps in chapter 4. Begin by sewing or gluing the finger-pressed angles to their background strips. Transfer the completed strip sets to the foundation, and use a glue stick to adhere them in place. Try to keep the angled bluff/hillside strips in close proximity to one another; remember to take into account the ¼" (6mm) seam allowance when you place the strips.

If you choose to glue the angles in place, stitch them down before going on to step 5.

5 With right sides together, fold and sew along the drawn grid lines, making sure to double-check that none of the fabrics have bunched up under the foundation before you sew. Use a large needle and tiny stitches. Tear away the foundation from the seam allowances and press the seams.

6 Following the manufacturer's instructions, press fusible web to the wrong side of the branch fabric, florals, scrap of green fabric and leaf fabrics.

7 Trace the tissue patterns onto the dull side of the freezer paper. Cut out the branches and press them to the right side of the branch fabric. Trace around the pattern and cut out the branches. (Save the freezer paper patterns—they can be used multiple times!)

8 Arrange the branches on the quilt top and fuse them in place.

9 Cut out the leaves, flowers and stems. Arrange and fuse them in place.

10 Use a white highlighting marker and a dark brown marker to shade and highlight the branches.

11 Square up the quilt top. Cut the inner border strips 1¼" (3.2cm) wide and the outer border strips 3½" (8.9cm) wide. Measure your finished quilt top to determine the lengths of the border strips, because your quilt may finish with slightly different dimensions than mine. Sew the borders to the quilt top. Tear away the rest of the foundation.

12 Referring to chapter 6, layer, baste and quilt. You can stitch down the appliqués as part of the quilting process or by using monofilament thread and stitching before you add the backing fabric. Add binding to finish.

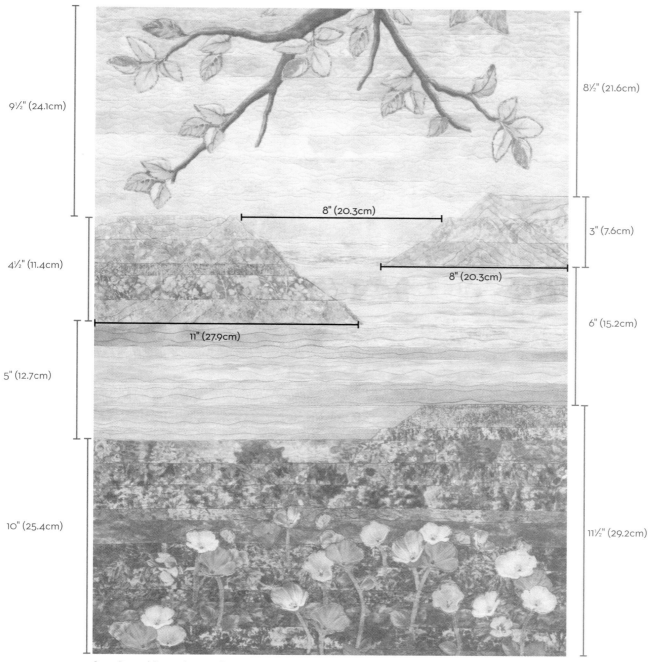

9½" (24.1cm)

4½" (11.4cm)

5" (12.7cm)

10" (25.4cm)

8½" (21.6cm)

3" (7.6cm)

6" (15.2cm)

11½" (29.2cm)

8" (20.3cm)

8" (20.3cm)

11" (27.9cm)

Strip-Pieced Spring Layout Diagram
19½ × 29 (49.5cm × 73.7cm) interior finished measurements

Strip-Pieced Fall

26½" × 36½" (67.3cm × 92.7cm)

This quilt is a variation of *Strip-Pieced Spring* (page 68) and is designed to be a companion piece to it.

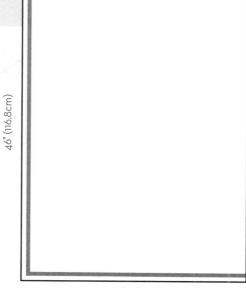

46" (116.8cm)

22" (55.9cm)
Draw plumb lines on the foundation

Materials

22" × 46" (55.9cm × 116.8cm) lightweight, tear-away foundation

⅓ yard (.3m) dark amber, brown and rust foreground fabrics

⅓ yard (.3m) water fabrics

¼ yard (.2m) lighter amber, brown and tan island fabrics

⅓ yard (.3m) sky fabrics

Brown fabric scraps to make the branches

¼ yard (.2m) fall leaf fabrics

¼ yard (.2m) foliage fabrics (ferns, etc.)

⅛ yard (.1m) inner border fabric

½ yard (.5m) outer border and binding fabric

Batting

1 yard (.9m) backing fabric

Supplies

1 yard (.9m) of 18"-wide (45.7cm) paper-backed fusible web for appliqués

2 yards (1.8m) of 18"-wide (45.7cm) fusible web for quilt basting

Glue stick

Freezer paper

White highlighting marker

Dark brown dye or fabric marker

Tissue patterns: Branch 1, Branch 2

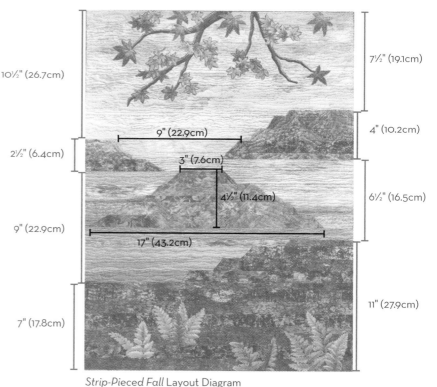

10½" (26.7cm)

2½" (6.4cm)

9" (22.9cm)

7" (17.8cm)

9" (22.9cm)

3" (7.6cm)

4½" (11.4cm)

17" (43.2cm)

7½" (19.1cm)

4" (10.2cm)

6½" (16.5cm)

11" (27.9cm)

Strip-Pieced Fall Layout Diagram
19½" × 29" (49.5cm × 73.7cm) interior finished measurements

Instructions

Follow the same directions as for the *Strip-Pieced Spring* landscape (page 68), but this time create bluffs with water on both sides. This makes for a slightly more difficult landscape to construct, but still fairly simple. Notice that some of the angled slopes in this quilt are more gradual (approximately 30°) and are just as easy to finger press and sew (See chapter 4 for details.) Since you are learning to use a tear-away foundation to piece, I recommend learning to glue these simple angles in place now before taking on the more challenging projects.

Follow the instructions for *Strip-Pieced Spring*, adding fall leaves and ferns instead of flowers.

Wildflowers by the Sea

24" × 32" (61cm × 81.3cm)

This fat-quarter-friendly landscape is a great project for learning how to combine strips by fusing them to a foundation. All these strips are straight. There will be no seam allowances to add in when designing this quilt. What you see is what the finished picture will look like. Instead of piecing any angles to create steep slopes, simply cut the end of the strip into the desired shape.

Look carefully and you can see how there are tiny narrow strips of water layered with wider, rocky bluff strips to the left. This is easy to create. For example, if the bluff strip is 1¼" (3.2cm) wide, then two ½" (1.3cm) strips and one ¼" (6mm) strip can be cut to fill the width on the water side.

Materials

18" × 26" (45.7cm × 66cm) fusible tricot interfacing for foundation (do not buy the kind with little dots of glue)

⅓ yard (.3m) golden brown foreground fabrics

⅓ yard (.3m) water fabrics (include lavenders, blues and whites)

¼ yard (.2m) rock bluff fabric

¼ yard (.2m) white and yellow flowers fabric

Scraps of light and dark green fabrics for the stems 4"–11" (10.2cm–27.9cm) tall butterfly image for appliqué

Scraps of fabric for the back of the butterfly

⅓ yard (.3m) inner border and binding fabric

½ yard (.5m) outer border fabric

Batting

1 yard (.9m) backing fabric

Supplies

1½ yards (1.4m) of 18"-wide (45.7cm) paper-backed fusible web for appliqués

2 yards (1.8m) of 18"-wide (45.7cm) fusible web for quilt basting

Instructions

1 Cut the foundation piece. With the fusible side up, lightly tape the corners to a smooth, flat surface on which you can use an iron. (I use a piece of plywood or an old card table.)

2 Cut the strips of darker foreground fabrics. I usually start at the bottom of my designs and work up. Cut a variety of strip widths; some can be 1½" (3.8cm), some ½" (1.3cm), etc. (Remember, these are finished sizes; there will be no piecing.)

Arrange these on the foundation, slightly overlapping the edges and filling the whole width. Measure the distance from the bottom of the foundation to the top of your design to help keep straight rows straight from one edge of the quilt to the other. (See photograph on page 45 in chapter 4.)

Every couple of rows, lightly press the strips with a medium-hot iron to activate enough of the glue so the strips won't shift when bumped.

3 Cut out the strips that will make the rocky bluff shapes. Arrange these and lightly press them to hold them in place.

4 Fill in the water strips. Look at the project picture for ideas about arranging narrow lavender and white strips to create the illusion of light on the water. Once again, measure carefully from top to bottom and lightly fuse in place as you go.

5 Continue building the picture, bringing in deep blue fabrics. I did not make a careful distinction between the sky and water in this quilt. If you would like to do so, go right ahead!

6 When the image is complete, press with a hot iron. Use steam and a pressing cloth to permanently fuse the strips.

7 Trim the quilt edges, making sure the corner edges are 90° angles and the length and width are even throughout.

8 Following the manufacturer's instructions, press fusible web to the wrong side of the white flowers, butterfly and green stem fabrics.

9 Cut out long, slightly curving green stems using a rotary cutter or scissors. They should be in assorted lengths and widths—longer stems can be 11" (27.9cm), shorter ones 4" (10.2cm). Stems should not be thicker than ⅜" (1.0cm) on the bottom.

10 Arrange the stems on the quilt top. Cut out individual white flowers and arrange them on top. Add more stems over some of the flowers and build a little garden. Fuse in place.

11 Cut out a butterfly and fuse it to the tiny fabric scrap for its underside. Trim off the edges. Arrange the butterfly and sew it in place using black thread and stitching down the edges of the body only. The wings will pop out a bit and make it look three-dimensional.

12 Square up the quilt top. Cut the inner border strips 1" (2.5cm) wide and the outer border strips 3½" (8.9cm) wide. Measure the finished quilt top to determine the lengths of the border strips, because your quilt may finish with slightly different dimensions than mine. Sew the borders to the quilt top.

13 Referring to chapter 6, layer, baste and quilt. Be sure to stitch down the edges of the strips and appliqués (see page 45, step 4). When you bind the quilt, create a wider binding (1½" [3.8cm]) if desired.

15" (38.1cm)

2½" (6.4cm)

7½" (19.1cm)

3" (7.6cm)

4" (10.2cm)

8½" (21.6cm)

7½" (19.1cm)

6" (15.2cm)

2½" (6.4cm)

10½" (26.7cm)

12" (30.5cm)

Layout Diagram

17½" × 25½" (44.5cm × 64.8cm) interior finished measurements

Sailing

34" × 43" (86.4cm × 109.2cm)

This quilt is created using two sections of a fusible interfacing. After each section is finished, the two sections are stitched together. Use bright, fun colors, and mix and match batiks and landscape prints—play! I purposely used busy prints to create this quilt; even the water is made using small floral fabrics. Nothing in this landscape needs to look completely real.

Materials

Two 19½" × 29" (49.5cm × 73.7cm) sections of fusible tricot interfacing for foundation (Do not buy the kind with little dots of glue.)

½ yard (.5m) sky fabrics (choose varying values of yellows, blues, apricots, lavenders, etc.)

⅓ yard (.3m) hill fabrics

¼ yard (.2m) green foreground fabrics

⅓ yard (.3m) water fabrics

10" × 15" (25.4cm × 38.1cm) piece of white print for the sails, mast and boat base

8" (20.3cm) square scrap of yellow fabric for the sail stripes

2" × 6" (5.1cm × 15.2cm) scrap of light brown wood grain print for the sailboat cabin

Gray scrap fabric for the cabin windows

Two 6" × 3" (15.2cm × 7.6cm) pieces of white tulle for the reflections

¾ yard (.7m) border and binding fabric

Batting

1½ yards (1.4m) backing fabric

Supplies

1 yard (.9m) of 18"-wide (45.7cm) paper-backed fusible web for appliqués

3 yards (2.7m) of 18"-wide (45.7cm) fusible web for quilt basting

Bo-Nash Bonding Powder

Brown dye or fabric marker

Glue stick

Tissue patterns: Sail 1, Sail 2, Boat Base, Cabin

Instructions

1 Cut out the two foundation pieces. With the fusible side up, lightly tape the corners of one piece to a smooth, flat surface that you can iron on. (I use a piece of plywood or an old card table.)

2 Cut strips of fabric, varying the widths from ½"–1½" (1.3cm–3.8cm). Starting at the bottom of the interfacing foundation, arrange the green meadow strips. Following the instructions for fusible interfacing construction on page 45, arrange and lightly press the strips in place, measuring from bottom to top as you go to achieve straight lines.

3 Next, add the blue strips, keeping the darker values toward the bottom of the quilt. Lightly press as you go, continuing to measure from bottom to top. After the bottom of the quilt is completed, fuse with steam and a pressing cloth. Set aside.

4 Tape down the second section of interfacing in the same way as the first and begin building purple hills at the bottom. Simply cut off the ends of the strips to create angled slopes. Lightly press as you go and be sure to measure from bottom to top as you design to maintain straight strips.

5 Next, create the sky. In strip sets where the sky meets the hills, cut the end of the sky strip to match the hill angle and tuck the tip of the sky strip beneath the hill strip. Lightly press the strips in place as you design. When this section is completed, fuse with steam using a pressing cloth.

6 Trim each foundation section, making sure you have 90° corners. Sew the land-and-sky section to the water section.

7 Create the boat using the sailboat pattern pieces. Trace the wrong side of the sails and the boat base onto paper-backed fusible web. Press the fusible web to the wrong side of the white fabric. Before cutting out the sails and the boat base, cut a 9" (22.9cm) long skinny mast from the white fabric. The bottom should measure ¼" (6mm) wide, and it should taper slightly toward the top.

Cut out the boat base.

Press fusible web to the wrong side of the yellow scrap and cut ¾" (1.9cm) strips. Peel off the paper and arrange the strips across the remaining white fabric. (Look at the project picture as needed.) Lightly fuse them to the white fabric and cut out the sails. Trim the ends flush with the sail edges. Fuse using steam.

Trace the wrong side of the sailboat cabin pattern to the back side of the paper-backed fusible web. Press the fusible web to the wrong side of the light brown scrap for the sailboat cabin. Cut out the cabin.

8 Arrange the sailboat parts on the water. Fuse them in place using steam and a pressing cloth.

9 Use the brown marker to lightly shade some brown trim along the top and bottom of the sailboat and create a darker brown base to the cabin. Cut two tiny oval windows from gray scraps and attach with a glue stick.

10 Following the instructions on page 54 for using Bo-Nash Bonding Powder, fuse together two layers of white tulle. Cut out long, wavy strips and layer them under the boat to create reflections. Use bonding powder to secure the tulle strips in place. Use a fiberglass pressing sheet and medium-hot iron to press in place. Be careful not to melt the tulle!

11 Square up the quilt top. Cut your outer border strips 3½" (8.9cm) wide. Measure your finished quilt top to determine the lengths of the border strips, because your quilt may finish with slightly different dimensions than mine. Sew on the border.

12 Referring to chapter 6, layer, baste and quilt. Be sure to stitch down the edges of your strips (see page 45, step 4). I meander stitched the foreground and quilted long, wavy horizontals in the sky and water. Add binding to finish.

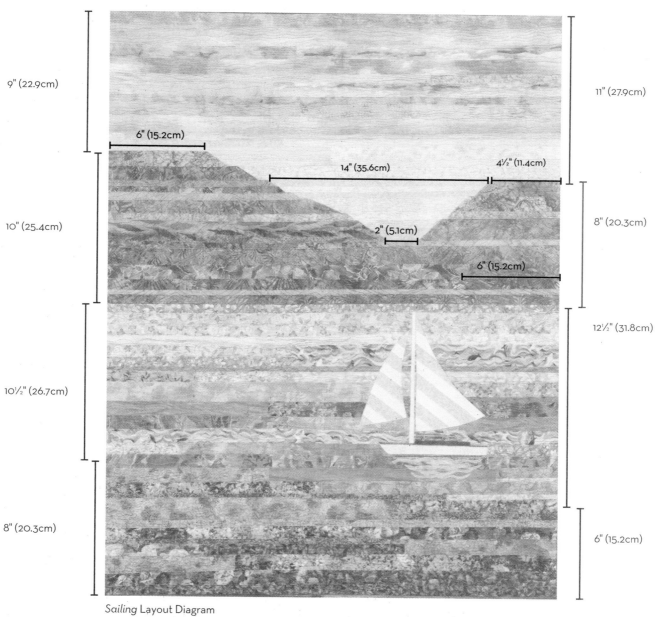

9" (22.9cm)

11" (27.9cm)

6" (15.2cm)

14" (35.6cm)

4½" (11.4cm)

10" (25.4cm)

8" (20.3cm)

2" (5.1cm)

6" (15.2cm)

12½" (31.8cm)

10½" (26.7cm)

8" (20.3cm)

6" (15.2cm)

Sailing Layout Diagram
29" × 37½" (73.7cm × 95.3cm) interior finished measurements

Foggy Spring

35½" × 43" (90.2cm × 109.2cm)

Foggy Spring and *Foggy Fall* (page 86) have a lovely abstract nature. Using simple, straight strips and gray-toned fabrics, *Foggy Spring* captures the feel of early spring on a rainy day. This quilt utilizes finished ¼" (6mm) strips in the design. This is a hard strip to sew accurately, so I encourage you to use a tear-away foundation to piece this quilt. Refer to chapter 4 (page 38) for more information on accurately sewing these narrow strips.

Materials

46" × 35" (116.8cm × 88.9cm) lightweight, tear-away foundation

1 yard (.9m) mixed gray background fabrics (ranging from light to medium values and in mixed tones with hints of greens and blues)

⅛ yard (.1m) mixed green fabrics for the foreground

⅛ yard (.1m) light gray blue batik fabrics for the sky areas

¼ yard (.2m) medium purple fabric for the highlighting strips

⅓ yard (.3m) brown and charcoal wood grain prints (I used only two prints because the wrong side of my fabrics worked for the lighter color tree trunks.)

⅓ yard (.3m) green leaf fabrics

¼ yard (.2m) purple flower fabrics

⅜ yard (.3m) inner border and binding fabric

½ yard (.5m) outer border fabric

Batting

1⅓ yards (1.2m) backing fabric

Supplies

1 yard (.9m) of 18"-wide (45.7cm) paper-backed fusible web for appliqués

3 yards (2.7m) of 18"-wide (45.7cm) fusible web for quilt basting

35" (88.9cm)
46" (116.8cm)
Draw plumb lines on the foundation

Tip

A gradated gray print like the one shown here makes creating the background a snap. If you can find a fabric like this, buy at least ½ yard (.5m) and mix in a few other grays.

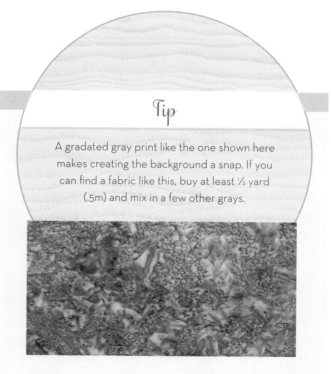

Instructions

1 Press the tear-away foundation to remove any wrinkles, then draft the plumb lines. Though this may seem counterintuitive, orient the foundation so the fold-and-sew lines run parallel to the 35" (88.9cm) side with the long 46" (116.8cm) side perpendicular to them. This is because the height of the pieced landscape is 35" (88.9cm), and the longer 46" (116.8cm) side will be needed to piece all the seam allowances. After the plumb lines are drawn, draw in the fold-and-sew lines. Starting at the left side of the foundation, draw a repeating pattern of three 1½"-wide (3.8cm) strips, one ¾"-wide (1.9cm) strip and one 2"-wide (5.1cm) strip. Repeat this pattern along the entire width of your foundation.

2 Cut and arrange your strips; keep the lighter gray and blue portions near the top and the greener foliage portions near the bottom. (Remember to cut the strips ⅛" [3mm] narrower than the drawn fold-and-sew column widths). Follow the project picture as needed and sew each strip set as you go, including sewing all angles.

3 Transfer each completed strip set to your foundation following the construction techniques outlined in chapter 4 (page 40). Fold and sew along the drawn lines; use a large needle and tiny stitches. Press and tear away the foundation from the seam allowances.

4 Press fusible web to the wrong side of the leaf and flower fabrics.

5 Cut out the leaves and flowers, remove the paper backing and arrange them on the quilt top. Fuse them in place.

6 Square up the quilt top. Cut the inner border strips 1¼" (3.2cm) wide and the outer border strips 4¼" (10.8cm) wide. Measure the finished quilt top to determine the lengths of the border strips, because your quilt may finish with slightly different dimensions than mine. Sew the borders to the quilt top. Tear away the rest of the foundation.

7 Referring to chapter 6, layer, baste and quilt. Add curlicue vines and loops in purple thread near and around the flowers. Stitch down the appliqués during the quilting process or before adding the backing. After the quilting is completed, add contrasting binding.

Note

The strip pattern on this quilt is more complicated than the earlier strip-pieced projects. This is because one of the thicker strips is a tree trunk and the rest of the trunks are spread out randomly.

Foggy Spring Quilting Detail

35½" × 43" (90.2cm × 109.2cm)

Foggy Fall turned out so well that, although it is simple, it is one of my favorite quilts. The colors and the way they work together capture those gray fall days when the deciduous trees are in full color; their red and gold leaves stand out and glow against the muted forest backdrop.

Materials

46" × 35" (116.8cm × 88.9m) lightweight, tear-away foundation

1¼ yards (1.1m) mixed gray background fabrics (ranging from light to medium values and in mixed tones with hints of greens and warm golden tans)

¼ yard (.2m) mixed green fabrics for the foreground

¼ yard (.2m) medium golden rust fabrics for the highlighting strips

⅓ yard (.3m) brown and charcoal wood grain prints (I used only two prints because the wrong side of my fabrics worked for the lighter color tree trunks.)

½ yard (.5m) fall leaf fabrics

⅜ yard (.3m) inner border and binding fabric

½ yard (.5m) outer border fabric

Batting

1⅓ yards (1.2m) backing fabric

Supplies

1 yard (.9m) of 18"-wide (45.7cm) paper-backed fusible web for appliqués

3 yards (2.7m) of 18"-wide (45.7cm) fusible web for quilt basting

35" (88.9cm)

46" (116.8cm)

Draw plumb lines on the foundation

Instructions

1 Press your foundation to remove any wrinkles, and draft your plumb lines. Follow the directions for *Foggy Spring* (page 84), orienting the foundation so the vertical fold-and-sew lines run parallel to the 35" (88.9cm) width. This quilt uses the same repeating order of strips as *Foggy Spring*, but starts out slightly differently so that when the quilts hang side by side, the trees aren't in the same positions. Therefore, begin on the left side by drawing in two 1½"-wide (3.8cm) strips, one ¾"-wide (1.9cm) strip and one 2"-wide (5.1cm) strip. From there, draw in a repeating pattern of three 1½"-wide (3.8cm) strips, one ¾"-wide (1.9cm) strip and one 2"-wide (5.1cm) strip; continue to repeat this pattern of repeating widths along the remaining width of the foundation. End with one 1½"-wide (3.8cm) strip.

2 Follow the instructions for *Foggy Spring* to finish sewing this quilt top. Use fall leaves instead of green leaves and flowers. After the border fabrics are sewn on, add a few leaves to the border area if desired.

3 Quilt the project using meander stippling. Bring in a darker, variegated, contrasting thread in places around the fall leaves if desired.

22" × 33" (55.9 × 83.8)

To make this quilt top, you'll free-form cut bright meadow fabrics to create the foreground, background road and hills. Use straight strips of pastel yellows and blues to create the sky.

Materials

17" × 28½" (43.2cm × 72.4cm) piece of tricot fusible interfacing for foundation (Do not buy the kind with the little dots of glue.)

¼ yard (.2m) sky fabrics

¼ yard (.2m) lower (foreground) meadow fabrics

¼ yard (.2m) upper meadow fabric

¼ yard (.2m) purple hill fabrics (some with green hues, some with pink hues)

¼ yard (.2m) tan road fabric

⅛ yard (.1m) foliage (to add along the road and fence and between the meadow and hills)

⅛ yard (.1m) tiny red and white flowers

Scrap of brown fabric for the tree

Scraps of light, medium and dark green and light blue for the tree canopy collage

3" × 2" (7.6cm × 5.1cm) scrap fabric for the fence rail posts

12" (30.5cm) square of white, yellow or light blue fine tulle

⅜ yard (.3m) inner border fabric and binding

½ yard (.5m) outer border fabric

Batting

¾ yards (.7m) backing fabric

Supplies

1 yard (.9m) of 18"-wide (45.7cm) paper-backed fusible web for appliqués

2 yards (1.8m) of 18"-wide (45.7cm) fusible web for quilt basting

Freezer paper

Sulky Super Solvy

Tissue patterns: Tree, Lower Meadow, Road, Upper Meadow, Hills 1–8

Glue stick or Bo-Nash Bonding Powder (optional)

Instructions

1 Trace the patterns onto the freezer paper.

2 Create the lower meadow portion of your landscape. Freehand cut strips and clumps of meadow fabrics and arrange them to fill your pattern's shape. Lightly fuse these fabrics in place.

3 Cut the road pattern out of the freezer paper and press it to the right side of the road fabric. Cut out the road and place it on the foundation above the meadow. (My road is created using free-form cut strips of fabric and thread painting to blend the strips together. You may choose to do this instead of using one road print.) When you are satisfied with the road, lightly fuse it in place.

4 Cut out the upper meadow from the freezer paper. Press this to the right side of the upper meadow fabric and cut it out. Arrange the upper meadow above the road and lightly fuse it in place.

5 Cut out and arrange the hills as described in step 4, working from the bottom up and slightly overlapping fabrics to cover the interfacing. Cut slightly larger patches as necessary, adjusting the pieces as you go. Lightly fuse the bottoms of the hills in place, but do not fuse the top edges.

6 Cut strips of sky fabrics. Strip widths can range from ½"–1¼" (1.3cm–3.2cm). Place lighter strips toward the horizon line and darker strips toward the top. Lightly fuse the strips in place.

7 When you are satisfied with the design, fuse the strips to the foundation using steam and a pressing cloth.

8 Trace the wrong side of the tree pattern to the paper side of the fusible web. Press the fusible web to the wrong side of the tree fabric and cut out the tree. Arrange the tree on the quilt top and fuse in place.

9 Create a leaf collage using the Sulky Super Solvy, following the instructions on pages 52–53. Use the tulle as a base and cut snippets from green and blue print scraps. Keep these snippets tiny—no bigger than ¼" (6mm).

10 After the collage is created and dry, cut out random curvy shapes. Use a glue stick, Bo-Nash Bonding Powder or bits of fusible web to adhere these shapes to the tree branches to create a canopy.

11 Press fusible web to the wrong side of the flower, fence post and foliage fabrics. Cut out flowers and fuse them in the meadow. Cut out, arrange and then fuse fence posts (each about ¼" [6mm] thick). Cut out bits of foliage and fuse them along the roadside and near the back of the meadow.

12 Square up the quilt top. Cut the inner border strips 1" (2.5cm) wide and the outer border strips 3¼" (8.3cm) wide. Measure the finished quilt top to determine the lengths of the border strips, because your quilt may finish with slightly different dimensions than mine. Sew the borders to the quilt top.

13 Referring to chapter 6, layer, baste and quilt. The edges of the patches and strips will need to be stitched down, as will the edges of the collage. Quilt the roadway using variegated threads, stitching down the hill and back up. You can add patches of green thread work here and there as desired. The sky is quilted using a long, horizontal zigzag stitch pattern in a variegated thread. The wire fence rails are stitched using a brown or dark gray thread; quilt them by going back and forth over the same stitching line to create the thick wire. Bind the quilt to finish.

A Pastoral Quilting Detail

27" × 28½"(68.6cm × 72.4cm)

This pretty little quilt is only tricky to create if you choose to be very fussy when lining up the hillsides. You'll have to take into account the ¼" (6mm) seam allowance while lining up your strips if you want matching angles (see pages 40–41 for help with this). I chose to create a fall companion to this quilt (pictured on page 95). If you would like to do the same, use the same pattern pieces, but substitute fall leaves for the green leaves and flowers.

Materials

22" × 43" (55.9cm × 109.2cm) lightweight, tear-away foundation

⅛ yard (.1m) foreground fabrics

⅛ yard (.1m) meadow fabrics

⅛ yard (.1m) hill fabrics

⅓ yard (.3m) sky fabrics

⅛ yard (.1m) medium brown fabric for the tree branch

¼ yard (.2m) flowers and leaf fabrics

⅛ yard (.1m) inner border fabric

½ yard (.5m) outer border fabric and binding

Batting

1 yard (.9m) backing fabric

Supplies

1 yard (.9m) of 18"-wide (45.7cm) paper-backed fusible web for appliqués

2 yards (1.8m) of 18"-wide (45.7cm) fusible web for quilt basting

Fine-tipped marker

Freezer paper

Tissue pattern: Branch

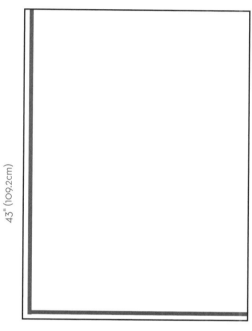

43" (109.2cm)

22" (55.9cm)

Draw plumb lines on the foundation

Instructions

1 Press the foundation to remove any wrinkles, and draft the plumb lines. Add the fold-and-sew lines, drawing them parallel to the 22" (55.9cm) width. Draw a repeating pattern of one 1½"-wide (3.8cm) strip, one 1¼"-wide (3.2cm) strip and one ¾"-wide (1.9cm) strip. Draw eleven full sets of this pattern but leave off the last ¾" (1.9cm) strip at the top. You will not fill the entire length of your foundation for this quilt.

2 Cut out and arrange the strips on your design wall, remembering to cut strips ⅛" (3mm) narrower than your drawn fold-and-sew lines.

3 Referring to the directions in chapter 4 (page 40), transfer the strips to the foundation. Sew together any simple strip segments, but don't sew the angles between the hills and the sky; glue these in place.

4 Stitch down the other mountainside/hill angles using matching or monofilament threads.

5 Fold and sew the strips together using a large needle and tiny stitches. Tear away the foundation from the seam allowances and press the quilt top flat. Trim and square up the quilt top.

6 Press fusible web to the wrong side of the branch fabric, the white flowers and the leaf fabrics.

7 Trace the branch pattern onto the freezer paper. Press the freezer paper to the right side of the branch fabric. Using a fine-tipped marker, trace around the freezer paper. Cut out the branch and arrange it on your quilt top. Fuse it in place with steam.

8 Cut out the flowers and leaves, remove the paper backing, arrange them and fuse in place.

9 Cut your inner border strips 1" (2.5cm) wide and your outer border at 3¼" (8.3cm) wide. Measure your finished quilt top to determine the lengths of the border strips, because your quilt may finish with slightly different dimensions than mine. Sew the borders to the quilt top. Tear away the rest of the foundation.

10 Referring to chapter 6, layer, baste and quilt, being sure to stitch down the edges of the appliqués. Bind the quilt to finish.

Layout Diagram
21" × 22½" (53.3cm × 57.2cm) interior finished

11" (27.9cm)

4" (10.2cm)

6" (15.2cm)

13" (33cm)

13½" (34.3cm)

4½" (10.8cm)

VARIATION: AFTER THE HARVEST

27" × 28½" (68.6cm × 72.4cm)

Poppies in the Rain and Mud

44½" × 43½" (113cm × 110.5cm)

This is a simple and fun landscape, and the colors make it a classy wall hanging. You can just piece these landscape strips—no need for a foundation to help keep these strips straight.

Materials

1 yard (.9m) mixed golden tan, warm beige and light beige fabrics

½ yard (.5m) blue and lavender fabrics

⅓ yard (.3m) deep earth-toned fabrics for the muddy foreground

¼ yard (.2m) mixed red and red-orange fabrics for the poppies

¼ yard (.2m) brown fabric for the stems

¼ yard (.2m) green leaf fabrics

10" (25.4cm) square of mottled black fabric for the center of the poppy flowers

½ yard (.5m) inner border and binding fabric

¾ yard (.7m) outer border fabric

Batting

2 yards (1.8m) backing fabric

Supplies

2 yards (1.8m) of 18"-wide (45.7cm) paper-backed fusible web for appliqués

4½ yards (4.1m) of 18"-wide (45.7cm) fusible web for quilt basting

Freezer paper

Tissue patterns: Poppies

Instructions

1 This quilt does not use a foundation. Cut and arrange the strips. The pattern for the strip layout starts by alternating between one 3½"-wide (8.9cm) finished strip and one 2"-wide (5.1cm) finished strip. Because these are the finished dimensions, cut the strips 4" (10.2cm) wide and 2½" (6.4cm) wide. You can see from the project picture that I used five 2" (5.1cm) strips in adjacent positions in the sky and ground areas. As you design, feel free to mix it up as you like. The strip-pieced section should finish approximately 36" × 35" (91.4cm × 88.9cm).

2 Sew the strip segments together. Then sew the strips together. Press the quilt top flat.

3 Press fusible web to the wrong side of the red poppy, red-orange poppy, black poppy center, brown stem and green leaf fabrics.

4 Trace the poppy patterns on freezer paper. Cut out the flowers and press the freezer paper to the right side of the red and red-orange fabrics. Cut out the poppies. You will notice that the flower patterns have a middle "petal" line separating the upper and lower flower petals. You can cut along this petal line and create some poppies with red-orange tops and red bottoms for variety. Cut out and add the black centers to your flowers. Make sure they overlap the middle of the petals, then fuse them in place.

5 Cut out long, skinny stems; some of these can be bent like the flower is falling over. Remove the paper backing from the stems, flowers and leaves; arrange them and fuse in place. Cut out squiggly red shapes to mimic the look of distant poppies. Fuse in place.

6 Cut the inner border strips 1¼" (3.2cm) wide and the outer border 4" (10.2cm) wide. Measure the finished quilt top to determine the lengths of the border strips, because your quilt may finish with slightly different dimensions than mine. Sew the borders to the quilt top.

7 Referring to chapter 6, layer, baste and quilt. Using a decorative red thread, topstitch the poppy petals. Then echo quilt the flower shapes. Quilt long, parallel vertical lines above the poppy flowers in a neutral thread. Meander quilt the muddy foreground, but add texture by creating stems, veins and leaves as you free-motion quilt the space between the flowers and the foreground. Bind the quilt to finish.

Poppies in the Rain and Mud Quilting Detail

Birches and Virginia Creeper

40" × 47½" (101.6cm × 120.7cm)

This is a simple yet dramatic quilt, and you can use a wide variety of fabrics to string piece the background blocks. Mix in landscape prints for extra texture, and use bold fall prints as the first fabric placed across the center diagonal of each block. The tree trunks are not fused in place—they are appliquéd and lightly stuffed with batting to make them pop off the background.

Materials

Tear-away foundation, cut into eighty 4¼" (10.8cm) squares and forty 4½" (11.4cm) squares

2½ yards (2.3m) of strips and scraps in greens, autumn rusts, golden tans, browns and blues in a variety of values

½ yard (.5m) birch trunk and branch fabrics (These do not have to be the same fabric. You can use gray and charcoal for the branches. Also make sure the bark print is oriented correctly along the length of the tree.)

⅓ yard (.3m) red leaf print

¼ yard (.2m) inner border fabric

⅓ yard (.3m) binding fabric

Batting, including 2 strips of batting place under the tree trunks

2 yards (1.8m) backing fabric

Supplies

1 yard (.9m) of 18"-wide (45.7cm) paper-backed fusible web for appliqués

4 yards (3.7m) of 18"-wide (45.7cm) fusible web for quilt basting

Spray starch

Freezer paper

Gray and black fabric dye markers (optional but highly recommended)

Tissue patterns: Trunk 1, Trunk 2, Branches 1–5

Instructions

1 String piece the 4¼" (10.8cm) background blocks. Keep the lighter and medium values together. Arrange the lighter finished blocks at the top of the design. Gradually bring in the darker values, and place these blocks toward the bottom of the design.

Piece the 4½" (11.4cm) blocks for the border.

2 Tear the foundation away from the pieced blocks. Spray with starch, press and square up each block. (Keep the slightly larger border blocks separate from the others.)

3 To form the quilt top, sew the blocks into rows, and the rows to each other. As you sew, press each row's seam allowances in opposite directions so when you sew rows together, you will have fewer lumps where the seam allowances join. Press the quilt top.

4 Trace the tree trunk tissue patterns onto the freezer paper. Cut out the tree trunk patterns leaving an extra 1"–2" (2.5cm–5.1cm) on the top and bottom of the paper. Press the paper to the right side of the trunk fabric. Cut the batting strips approximately ¼" (6mm) narrower than the trunk patterns.

5 Cut out the tree trunks leaving ⅓"–½" (8mm–1.3cm) of excess fabric along the edges. With the freezer paper still on top, turn and press the fabric edges under. Clip any curves as necessary.

6 Peel off the freezer paper and pin the tree trunks in place. Using monofilament thread and the stitch of your choice, stitch down one side of each tree. Open up each tree and insert a batting strip. The batting strips should be placed approximately ¼" (6mm) away from the top and bottom of the quilt top. Pin the trees closed and stitch down the remaining long sides.

7 Trace the branch patterns onto the freezer paper and cut them out.

8 Press the fusible web to the wrong side of the branch fabric and red leaf print.

9 Press the freezer paper branches to the right side of the prepared branch fabric and cut out the branches. Arrange the branches and fuse them in place.

10 Cut out and arrange the red leaves. Fuse them in place.

11 Using the gray dye marker, shade one side of each tree trunk and the underside of each branch. Use a darker gray or black marker as necessary to achieve the desired result.

12 Cut the inner border strips 1¼" (3.2cm) wide. Measure the finished quilt top to determine the lengths of the border strips, because your quilt may finish with slightly different dimensions than mine. Sew the inner border to the quilt top, stitching down the tops and bottoms of the tree trunks as you go.

13 Sew border blocks into four rows of ten blocks each, adjusting the seam allowances to fit the width and height of your quilt top. Sew the borders to the quilt top.

14 Referring to chapter 6, layer, baste and quilt. Because the print pattern for the string-pieced blocks is busy, stippling and meander quilting are all that are necessary for quilting the background. The tree trunks can be quilted in horizontal zigzags. Bind the quilt to finish.

Tip

Save the freezer paper branch patterns for future projects! I keep a big bag full of branches so I don't have to design branches for every project.

Birches and Virginia Creeper Quilting Detail

38" × 29" (96.5cm × 73.7cm)
In the collection of Sarah and Christopher Povlich.

I live in Wisconsin, and we love our barns! This whimsical quilt is easy to piece, and all the decorative embellishments are fused on after the quilt top is sewn together. You'll need all sorts of scraps in light to dark values. Be sure to look at the wrong side of your fabrics—their values might be just perfect for the look you are trying to achieve.

Materials

Tear-away foundation, cut into fifty-nine 5" (12.7cm) squares

¾ yard (.7m) mixed green fabrics for the foreground

1 yard (.9m) mixed blue fabrics for the sky (a ½ yard [.5m] of one gradated blue is recommended for blending value changes)

⅓ yard (.3m) barn fabric

Four scraps of flower and sun fabric

10" × 2" (25.4cm × 5.1cm) scrap for the green stems

Barn quilt block decoration (Fussy cut image from a print or use assorted tiny bright scraps for piecing [see step 8 for instructions].)

10" × 2" (25.4cm × 5.1cm) scrap of light gray fabric for the barn roof trim

3" (7.6cm) square scrap of mottled gray fabric for the barn windows

5" × 2" (12.7cm × 5.1cm) scrap of white fabric for the barn door trim

¼ yard (.2m) binding fabric or ½ yard (.5m) for back facing

Batting

1¼ yards (1.1m) backing fabric

Supplies

1 yard (.9m) of 18"-wide (45.7cm) paper-backed fusible web for appliqués

2½ yards (2.3m) of 18"-wide (45.7cm) fusible web for quilt basting

Spray starch

Freezer paper

Gray metallic permanent marker

White fabric dye marker

Black permanent marker

Glue stick

Water-soluble marking pen

Tissue patterns: Upper Roof, Lower Roof, Daisy, Sun

Instructions

1 Following the string-piecing instructions on page 46, string piece fifty-nine blocks on tear-away foundation. Piece these blocks with the strips running vertically or horizontally, not diagonally. Make twenty-four green blocks and thirty-five blue blocks. Mix in darker blue values for the sky blocks on top and lighter blue values for the sky blocks near the horizon line. (Using one gradated blue print can be very helpful in creating the blue sky.) When cutting strips to string piece, be sure to vary the widths to make the piecing more interesting. Cut strip widths from ¾"–1½" (1.9cm–3.8cm).

2 After the blocks are created, tear away the foundation. Spray with starch and press the blocks. Trim each block to 5" (12.7cm) square. Arrange the blocks on the design wall.

3 Cut out three 5" (12.7cm) squares of barn fabric for the lower story. Arrange them according to the project picture; these blocks fall below the horizon line. Cut out one 2½" × 5" (6.4cm × 12.7cm) strip of barn fabric and one 2½" (6.4cm) strip of light blue sky fabric. Sew these together to make one 5" (12.7cm) block; this is the middle story. Arrange the barn on the design wall. (The roof of the barn is fused in place after the blocks are stitched together.)

4 To form the quilt top, sew the blocks into rows, and sew the rows to each other. As you sew, press each row's seam allowances in opposite directions so when you sew rows together, you will have fewer lumps where the seam allowances join. Press the quilt top.

5 Press fusible web to the wrong side of the barn fabric, gray and white trim scraps, window scraps, flower and sun fabrics and green stem scraps.

6 Trace the barn roof tissue patterns onto the freezer paper. Cut them out and press the freezer paper to the right side of the barn fabric. (Make sure to keep the wood grain oriented vertically when creating the barn roof!) Cut out the roof pieces and arrange them on the quilt top. The roof may need to be adjusted slightly to fit the barn base. After you are satisfied, fuse the roof to the quilt top.

7 Cut narrow strips of gray and white trim and create the roofline and door trims. The door trim is ¼" (6mm) wide, and the gray roof trim is ⅜" (1cm) wide. Fuse the trim in place. Cut out little windows, roughly ⅞" × ¾" (2.2cm × 1.9cm). Fuse the windows in place.

8 Trace the flower and sun patterns on the freezer paper. Cut them out and press them to the right side of the prepared fabrics. Cut out the sun and the flowers. Fuse the flowers and sun on the quilt top.

From leftover bits of the green prints, messy cut a small, long garden to go at the base of the barn. Fuse or glue the garden in place.

Cut out skinny stems up to 8" (20.3cm) long. Arrange and fuse them in place. Bits of leftover flower fabric can be cut into tiny hearts and fused around the flowers.

The barn block decoration should be approximately 2¼" (5.7cm) square and can be created by using a fusible web or by fussy cutting a block from a preprinted fabric. If you wish to make this block, use ¼" (6mm) graph paper and draw out a quilt block. Trace it onto the paper side of the fusible web and cut out tiny squares and triangles to form the design. Arrange the fabric pieces on the side with the fusible adhesive and fuse the block. Then peel off the paper backing and fuse the decoration to the barn. I used a light blue marker to highlight the block's edges to set off the design.

9 Use a white marker to make the barn look weathered. Also use this marker to add smudges in the windows and to add highlights to the top of the gray trim on the barn roof. Use a gray metallic marker to create the windowpanes and edges. Use a black marker to create a shadow under the roof of the barn.

10 Referring to chapter 6, layer, baste and quilt. Use the freezer paper flower template to mark quilting lines in the sky with a water-soluble marking pen. Quilt these flowers with dark blue thread. Stipple the sun with bright yellow thread. As you meander and stipple the sky, add curly loops and tiny hearts.

Quilt the barn by stitching parallel lines every ⅓" (8mm) or so up and down the sides with a red variegated thread. Topstitch the tiny windows and panes with a contrasting light gray thread. Use the same thread to stitch the top part of the barn roof trim.

11 Sew on binding or back facing as desired.

I ♥ Wisconsin Quilting Detail

Spring Branches

47" × 52" (119.4cm × 132.1cm)

I used a complicated repeating strip pattern to piece the background of this quilt, so feel free to change the pattern if you would like. There are a wide variety of trunk sizes and only a few purple highlighting strips in this design. I created two of the tree trunks by placing bark strips in adjacent positions. This quilt was exhibited at the American Quilter's Society show in Grand Rapids, Michigan, in 2012.

Materials

Two 31" × 42" (78.7cm × 106.7cm) pieces of lightweight, tear-away foundation

1½ yards (1.4m) mixed green and batik prints

¼ yard (.2m) purple highlighting prints

½ yard (.5m) mixed brown bark prints

½ yard (.5m) brown branch fabric

¼ yard (.2m) brown fabric for the sapling

¼ yard (.2m) purple flowers print fabric

¼ yard (.2m) white flowers print fabric

¼ yard (.2m) green leaves print fabric

¼ yard (.2m) inner border fabric

⅝ yard (.6m) middle border and binding fabric

1½ yards (1.4m) outer border fabric

Batting

2½ yards (2.3m) backing fabric

Supplies

3 yards (2.7m) of 18"-wide (45.7cm) paper-backed fusible web for appliqués

4½ yards (4.1m) of 18"-wide (45.7cm) fusible web for quilt basting

Silver metallic permanent marker

Freezer paper

Tissue patterns: Branches 1–4

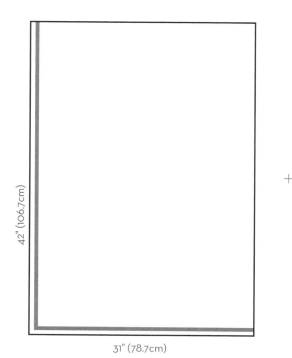
42" (106.7cm)
31" (78.7cm)

+

42" (106.7cm)
31" (78.7cm)

Draw plumb lines on the foundation pieces

Instructions

1 Press the foundation to remove any wrinkles, then draft the plumb lines. Draw the fold-and-sew lines so they run parallel to the 42" (106.7cm) length of the foundation on both sections.

While most of the strips are cut to finish at the same width for easier cutting, mixing in the ¼"- (6mm) and ½"-wide (1.3cm) finished highlighting strips at seemingly random intervals is trickier. If you follow my arrangement, the fold-and-sew lines should repeat the following pattern across the length of the foundation: one 1½"-wide (3.8cm) strip, one ¾"-wide (1.9cm) strip, two 1½"-wide (3.8cm) strips, one 1"-wide (2.5cm) strip, three 1½"-wide (3.8cm) strips and one 1"-wide (2.5cm) strip.

2 Cut out and arrange the strips, sewing each strip set as you go—nothing needs to line up. Mix in batiks and all-over forest prints to create a nicely textured background for the branches.

3 Follow the fold-and-sew construction directions in chapter 4. Before completing each section, however, sew the two pieces of foundation together. Do this by trimming off the right side of your first piece of foundation along the last fold-and-sew line, then trim off the left side of your second piece of foundation along the first fold-and-sew line. Sew the two sections together by lining up the two trimmed lines. Continue folding and sewing the rest of the quilt top. (When I join two sections, I usually fold and sew most of the rows in each section, but leave 3"–4" [7.6cm–10.2cm] unsewn on each side I'm going to join; this makes it easier to align the foundation sections accurately.) Finish the background using the fold-and-sew process. Use a large needle and tiny stitches. Tear the foundation from the seam allowances and press the quilt top.

4 Trace the branch tissue patterns onto the freezer paper. Cut out the branches. The long branch on the right and the one on the top left are the same branch; one is reversed.

5 Press the fusible web to the wrong side of the branch fabric, sapling fabric, purple flower fabric, green leaves fabric and white flower fabric.

6 Press the freezer paper branches to the right side of the branch fabric. Use the silver metallic marker to trace around the edges of the pattern onto the fabric and cut out the branches. Arrange the branches and fuse them in place.

7 Cut out the white flowers and leaves. Arrange them on the branches at the top of the design. Fuse them in place.

8 The saplings at the bottom were created by freehand cutting a few ¼" (6mm) curved strips of brown fabric. Follow the project picture and cut out a few long, curved saplings. Arrange these saplings in place. Cut out clumps of purple flowers, remove the backing and arrange them on and around the saplings. When you are satisfied, fuse everything in place.

9 Square up the quilt top. Cut the inner border strips 1"-wide (2.5cm), the middle border strips 1½"-wide (3.8cm) and the outer border strips 4"-wide (10.2cm). Measure your finished quilt top to determine the lengths of the strips, because your quilt may finish with slightly different dimensions than mine. Sew on the borders.

10 Referring to chapter 6, layer, baste and quilt, being sure to stitch down all appliqués. I stippled the background, stitching in the ditch around the flowers and leaves. I also added purple loops around the purple flowers. Bind the quilt to finish.

Spring Branches Quilting Detail

Wyoming Sunrise

48½" × 51" (123.2cm × 129.5cm)

This abstract, three-dimensional landscape is actually a lot easier than it looks. The strips only somewhat line up when creating the gray mountains and sun. The design is actually more interesting when the forest, meadow and foreground strips are jagged and uneven.

Materials

Two 33" × 42" (83.8cm × 106.7cm) sections of lightweight, tear-away foundation

¾ yard (.7m) light blue and lavender fabrics for the sky

½ yard (.5m) light to medium gray fabrics for the wide mountain strips

¼ yard (.2m) medium to dark blue and purple fabrics for the darker alternating mountain strips

⅛ yard (.1m) yellow fabrics for the sun

½ yard (.5m) dark brown and charcoal fabrics for the foreground

⅓ yard (.3m) light to medium green fabrics for the meadow

½ yard (.5m) allover tree prints

⅛ yard (.1m) red for the Indian paintbrush wildflowers

⅛ yard (.1m) green scrap for the flower stems and leaves

¼ yard (.2m) rocky/grassy scenic landscape print for the foreground appliqué

⅔ yard (.6m) of deep-toned reds, blues and golds for the narrow highlighting strips

¼ yard (.2m) inner border fabric

¼ yard (.2m) middle border fabric

1½ yards (1.4m) outer border and binding fabric

Batting

2½ yards (2.3m) backing fabric

Supplies

1 yard (.9m) of 18"-wide (45.7cm) paper-backed fusible web for appliqués

4½ yards (4.1m) of 18"-wide (45.7cm) fusible web for quilt basting

Glue stick

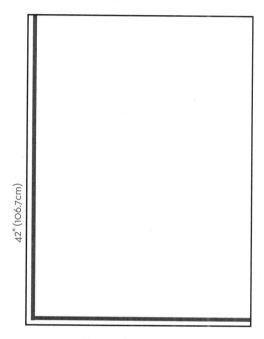

42" (106.7cm)

33" (83.8cm)

Draw plumb lines on both foundation pieces

42" (106.7cm)

33" (83.8cm)

Instructions

1 Press the foundation to remove any wrinkles, then draft the plumb lines. Add the fold-and-sew lines running parallel to the long 42" (106.7cm) side of the foundation. Start at the left side and draw a repeating pattern of one 1¾"-wide (4.4cm) strip, one 1¼"-wide (3.2cm) strip and one ¾"-wide (1.9cm) strip across the width of both foundation sections.

2 Arrange the strip segments vertically along a design wall, starting at the bottom of the design with the dark brown and charcoal fabrics. (Remember to cut the strips ⅛" (3mm) narrower than the drawn fold-and-sew lines when using a tear-away foundation to piece.)

3 Transfer the strip segments to the foundation. Some of the strips can be sewn together as you transfer them. If you want the gray mountain strips to line up like mine, don't sew these strip angles. Instead, glue them in place on the foundation, carefully arranging their positions to take into account the seam allowances. (See page 40 for more information on this technique.)

Stitch any glued angles to the foundation using monofilament or matching thread.

4 Follow the fold-and-sew construction directions in chapter 4. Before completing each section, however, sew the two pieces of foundation together. Do this by trimming off the right side of your first piece of foundation along the last fold-and-sew line, then trim off the left side of your second piece of foundation along the first fold-and-sew line. Sew the two sections together by lining up the two trimmed lines. Continue folding and sewing the rest of the quilt top. (When I join two sections, I usually fold and sew most of the rows in each section, but leave 3"–4" [7.6cm–10.2cm] unsewn on each side I'm going to join; this makes it easier to align the foundation sections accurately.) Finish the background using the fold-and-sew process. Use a large needle and tiny stitches. Tear the foundation from the seam allowances and press the quilt top.

5 Create a rock garden from the scenic landscape print. Use a glue stick or fusible web to adhere it to the bottom of the landscape.

6 Press paper-backed fusible web to the wrong side of the red and green fabrics to create the Indian paintbrush wildflowers. Cut out green stems and leaves from the green fabric and V shapes from the red fabric in varying sizes. Arrange the V shapes in rows to create the Indian paintbrush wildflowers. Fuse in place.

7 Use a decorative red thread to thread paint over each of the flowers' petals. Do the same with green thread over the flower leaves.

8 Square up the quilt top. Cut the inner border strips 1" (2.5cm) wide, the middle border strips 1½" (3.8cm) wide and the outer border strips 4½" (11.4cm) wide. Measure the finished quilt top to determine the lengths of the border strips, because your quilt may finish with slightly different dimensions than mine. Sew on the borders.

9 Referring to chapter 6, layer, baste and quilt. Quilt directly over the narrow highlighting strips and stipple or meander quilt the foreground and meadow. Quilt long crevasses down the mountain slopes and gentle horizontal meanders throughout the sky. Use a bright yellow thread to create a circular quilting pattern around and in the sun portion of the landscape. Bind the quilt to finish.

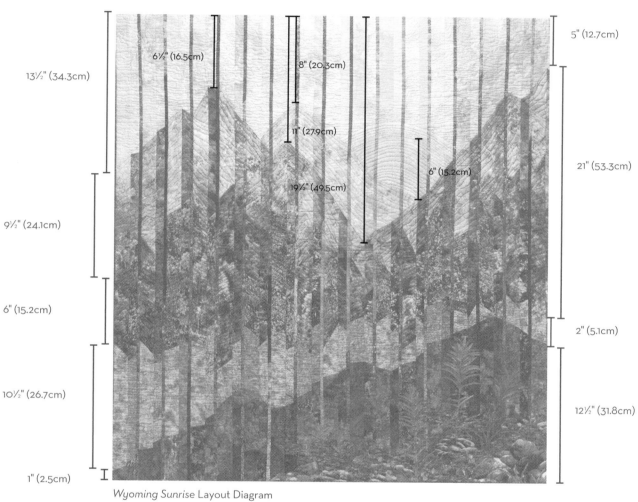

13½" (34.3cm)

9½" (24.1cm)

6" (15.2cm)

10½" (26.7cm)

1" (2.5cm)

6½" (16.5cm)

8" (20.3cm)

11" (27.9cm)

19½" (49.5cm)

6" (15.2cm)

5" (12.7cm)

21" (53.3cm)

2" (5.1cm)

12½" (31.8cm)

Wyoming Sunrise Layout Diagram
38" × 40½" (96.5cm × 102.9cm) interior finished measurements

Blue Ridge Mountain Sunset

41" × 34" (104.1cm × 86.4cm)

This dramatic sunset features backlit mountains and deep shadows—not to mention all my favorite colors! When I created this quilt, I followed a repeating pattern of strip widths, but I added in additional narrow highlighting strips for the sunset itself. Follow the project picture and, as you design, add in narrow ½" (1.3cm) strips of intense color and see what happens!

Materials

35" × 46" (88.9cm × 116.8cm) section of lightweight, tear-away foundation

⅓ yard (.3m) mixed sunset fabrics (warm colors in yellow, apricot, peach and magenta)

⅓ yard (.3m) mixed purple and lavender fabrics (medium-light to medium values) for the deep night sky

¾ yard (.7m) mixed blue-green, gray-blue and teal fabrics for the middle ground

¼ yard (.2m) mixed deep blue fabrics for the shadowed hill (bottom left)

¾ yard (.7m) mixed meadow green fabrics for the foreground

¼ yard (.2m) peach/pink flower print

¼ yard (.2m) small green leaves print

Two 11" (27.9cm) squares of white tulle

¼ yard (.2m) inner border fabric

¾ yard (.7m) outer border fabric and binding

Batting

1⅓ yards (1.2m) backing fabric

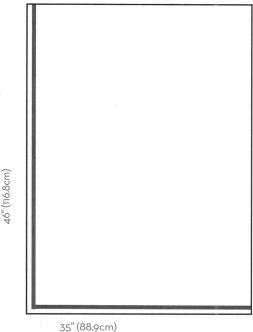

46" (116.8cm)

35" (88.9cm)

Draw plumb lines on the foundation

Supplies

1½ yards (1.4m) paper-backed fusible web (I recommend Steam-A-Seam for this project.)

3 yards (2.7m) of 18"-wide (45.7cm) fusible web for quilt basting

Instructions

1 Press the foundation to remove any wrinkles, then draft the plumb lines. The fold-and-sew lines run parallel to the 35" (88.9cm) width. Begin at the bottom and draft fold-and-sew lines up approximately half the height of the foundation. For this quilt, you will draft the rest of the fold-and-sew lines on the top of the foundation after the design is complete because you might want to vary the pattern of strips as you design the sunset. As you will notice, I used a regular strip pattern until I reached the portion of the landscape that included the sunset. If you find the perfect fabric (for example, one fabric with variegated stripes in light to intense golden yellows) you may not have to mix in additional ½" (1.3cm) strips of color like I did. (This is why this is an advanced project; you have to work a little harder to get the sunset right!) Therefore, from the bottom up, draw a repeating pattern of one 1½"-wide (3.8cm) strip, one 1¼"-wide (3.2cm) strip, one 1½"-wide (3.8cm) strip and one ¾"-wide (1.9cm) strip. Set the foundation aside.

2 Cut and arrange the strips. Remember to cut the strips ⅛" (3mm) narrower than your drawn fold-and-sew lines. Build the mountain ranges following the fabric placement diagram. When you get to the sunset, try adding in additional finished ½" (1.3cm) strips of color and don't be afraid to experiment! My sunset is made with a mix of finished ½" (1.3cm) strips, finished 1" (2.5cm) strips and finished ¼" (6mm) strips. After you are satisfied with your arrangement, pay attention to the strip widths and finish drafting your fold-and-sew lines accordingly. You will probably have to count your existing fold-and-sew rows so you know when to begin changing the pattern.

3 Follow the directions in chapter 4 (page 40) to transfer the strip segments to the foundation. The simple strip segments can be sewn, and the more complicated segments should be glued. (If you want the dark blue hillside to line up, glue those angles in place.)

4 Fold and sew your quilt top together. Tear away the foundation from the seam allowances and press the quilt top.

5 Press fusible web to the wrong side of your flower and leaf fabrics. Cut out flowers and leaves from the fabric. Arrange the flowers and leaves on your quilt top. (The sticky side of the Steam-A-Seam will help you arrange your mountain azaleas.) When you are satisfied, fuse them in place.

6 Layer the two pieces of white tulle and cut out five 10" (25.4cm) long rays. The rays should be cut in widths varying from 1¼"–1½" (3.2cm–3.8cm) wide. Carefully pin these double-layered rays to the quilt top. (Follow the project photograph for placement.) Stitch down the edges of the rays and remove the pins.

7 Square up the quilt top. Cut the inner border strips ¾" (1.9cm) wide and the outer border strips 3¾" (9.5cm) wide. Measure the finished quilt top to determine the lengths of the border strips, because your quilt may finish with slightly different dimensions than mine. Sew on the borders.

8 Referring to chapter 6, layer, baste and quilt. Be sure to stitch down the edges of your appliqués. With white thread, stitch long, parallel lines through the rays. Use variegated threads to quilt the rest of the quilt top. Bind the quilt to finish.

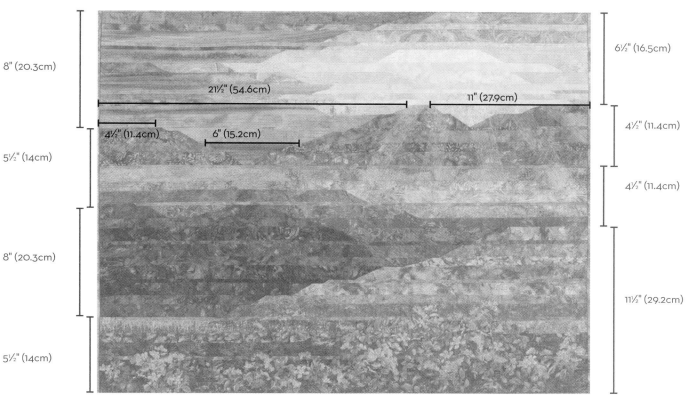

8" (20.3cm)

5½" (14cm)

8" (20.3cm)

5½" (14cm)

6½" (16.5cm)

4½" (11.4cm)

4½" (11.4cm)

11½" (29.2cm)

21½" (54.6cm)

11" (27.9cm)

4½" (11.4cm)

6" (15.2cm)

Blue Ridge Mountain Sunset Layout Diagram
33½" × 27" (85.1cm × 68.6cm) interior finished

Lone Cypress Tree

51" × 42" (129.5cm × 106.7cm)

The cypress tree and its rocky outcropping are the focal points in this coastal scene. Piecing the rocky outcropping is tricky, so don't sew the strip segments together for this part of the landscape; these angles will be glued down. The tree and the thread painting are easy to do. Simply stitch back and forth in long zigzags with a variegated green thread to complete the look.

Materials

Two 28" × 43" (71.1cm × 109.2cm) pieces of lightweight, tear-away foundation

¾ yard (.7m) blue water fabrics in a range of medium-light to medium-dark values

⅓ yard (.3m) dark green foliage and/or rock fabrics for the foreground

½ yard (.5m) medium-brown to light tan fabrics for the rocky outcropping

¼ yard (.2m) medium to light green foliage for the distant hills

⅓ yard (.3m) apricot and peach tones for the dawn

⅓ yard (.3m) light and medium blue fabrics for the sky

Scrap of brown fabric for the tree trunks

¼ yard (.2m) green foliage for the tree leaves (This print needs to have some light and medium flecks of gold or light green in it.)

¼ yard (.2m) inner border fabric

1½ yards (1.4m) outer border and binding fabric

Batting

2¼ yards (2.1m) backing fabric

Supplies

1 yard (.9m) of 18"-wide (45.7cm) paper-backed fusible web for appliqués

4 yards (3.7m) of 18"-wide (45.7cm) fusible web for quilt basting

Freezer paper

Glue stick

Silver metallic permanent marker

Tissue patterns: Tree Trunk 1, Tree Trunk 2

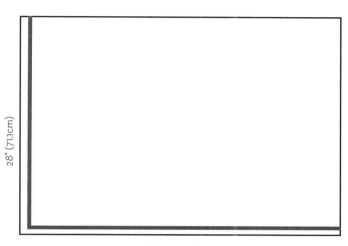

28" (71.1cm)

43" (109.2cm)

+

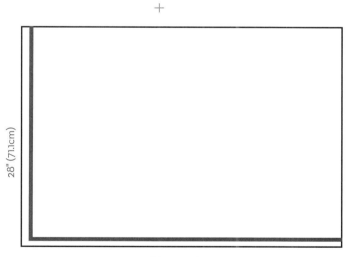

28" (71.1cm)

43" (109.2cm)

Draw plumb lines on both foundation pieces

Instructions

1 Press the foundation sections to remove any wrinkles, and draft the plumb lines. Then add the fold-and-sew lines running parallel to the 43" (109.2cm) long side of the foundation. Fill both sections of the foundation with this repeating pattern: one 2"-wide (5.1cm) strip, one 1½"-wide (3.8cm) strip, and one 1"-wide (2.5cm) strip.

2 Cut and arrange the strips on a design wall. Remember to cut the strips ⅛" (3mm) narrower than the drawn grid lines. Simple segments can be pieced while you are arranging them, but don't piece the rocky bluff area. Just pin those strips to the design wall.

3 Follow the directions in chapter 4 (page 40) to transfer the strip segments to the foundation. When you get to the rocky bluff, glue the blue ocean fabric in place and glue the tan rock angles over the top.

4 Follow the fold-and-sew construction directions in chapter 4. Before completing each section, however, sew the two pieces of foundation together. Do this by trimming off the top of your first piece of foundation along the last fold-and-sew line, then trim off the bottom of your second piece of foundation along the first fold-and-sew line. Sew the two sections together by lining up the two trimmed lines. Continue folding and sewing the rest of the quilt top. (When I join two sections, I usually fold-and-sew most of the rows in each section, but leave 3"–4" [7.6cm–10.2cm]) unsewn on each side I'm going to join; this makes it easier to align the foundation sections accurately.) Finish the background using the fold-and-sew process. Use a large needle and tiny stitches. Tear the foundation from the seam allowances and press the quilt top.

5 Press fusible web to the wrong side of your brown tree trunk and leafy green foliage fabrics.

6 Trace the tree trunk patterns onto the freezer paper. Cut out the tree trunks and press the freezer paper to the right side of the brown fabric. Trace around the trunks onto the fabric using a metallic marker and cut out the tree trunks.

7 From the foliage fabrics, cut out oblong, messy foliage shapes; cut in a few deep zigzags to mimic the branching habits of the cypress trees. Arrange the tree trunks and the foliage and fuse them in place.

8 Using a decorative green thread, lightly zigzag stitch back and forth over all the tree foliage. You don't need to fill in the area now—just stitch enough to hold everything down and add a bit of texture. You will be stitching the same way when you quilt the trees, so don't overdo it at this point.

9 Square up the quilt top. Cut the inner border strips 1" (2.5cm) wide and the outer border strips 4½" (11.4cm) wide. Measure the finished quilt top to determine the lengths of the border strips, because your quilt may finish with slightly different dimensions than mine. Sew on the borders.

10 Referring to chapter 6, layer, baste and quilt. The sky and water can be quilted using long, wavy horizontals. Meander or stipple quilt the foreground and rocky outcropping. Once again, thread paint back and forth over the foliage. Extend the stitching beyond the edges of the fabric to create a more feathery appearance. Create gentle bluff crevasses in the distant hills. Bind the quilt to finish.

8" (20.3cm)

4" (10.2cm)

5" (12.7cm)

8½" (21.6cm)

7" (17.8cm)

12" (30.5cm)

5" (12.7cm)

16½" (41.9cm)

4" (10.2cm)

11" (27.9cm)

4½" (11.4cm)

5½" (14cm)

20" (50.8cm)

Lone Cypress Tree Layout Diagram
41½" × 32½" (105.4cm × 82.6cm) interior finished

Dedication

So many thank-yous are needed here!

First, I'd like to thank my husband, Ted, for his continued support of my quilting addiction. It's just great knowing I get to live with, eat with, hike, camp and play with my number one fan. I'd like to thank Elizabeth, Peter and Teddy for their unknowing encouragement as they argue over which quilt will one day be theirs. And I'd like to thank my parents for stealing my best quilts for their own walls and keeping them out of my kids' hands.

Many thanks go to my editor, Kelly Biscopink, and designer, Kelly Pace. You both were wonderful to work with, and your hard work turned the manuscript into a thing of beauty.

To my contributing artists, I wish continued creative success. Thank you all so much for sharing your art with us in this book and online for all to enjoy. We have access to so much beauty and inspirational art because you all choose to share it with the world. Is it any wonder that the fiber art field is exploding with creativity? By making your works of art available, you encourage this generation and the next to reach for scissors and fabric to nurture their creative souls.

I would also like to offer my thanks to all my Facebook, Pinterest and blog fans and friends. Your comments and "Likes" mean a lot to me; they inspire and encourage me. In this new world of cyber relationships, you guys are the best. (Plus, I couldn't have named half of the quilts without you!)

Lastly but most importantly, I'd like to thank my Heavenly Father for making all these things possible.

All this earth
Could all that is lost ever be found?
Could a garden come up from this ground, at all?

All around
Hope is springing up from this old ground.
Out of chaos life is being found in You.

You make beautiful things.
You make beautiful things out of dust.
You make beautiful things out of us.

Into the darkness You shine.
Out of the ashes we rise.
There's no one like You.
None like You.

Song lyrics by Michael & Lisa Gungor and Chris Tomlin

Resources

Author

Cathy Geier
cathygeier.com
patchworksthatpraise.com
www.facebook.com/
patchworksthatpraise
www.pinterest.com/cathygeier/
http://cathygeier.blogspot.com/

Contributing Artists

Ann Brauer
6 Bridge Street
Shelburne Falls, MA 01370
ann@annbrauer.com
www.annbrauer.com

Coreen Zerr
3648 Glenoaks Drive
Nanaimo, BC V9T 5L3
Canada
www.coreenzerr.com

Denise Labadie
2827 Clear Creek Lane
Lafayette, CO 80026
denise.labadie@gmail.com
www.labadiefiberart.com

Elena Stokes
Clinton, NJ
www.elenastokes.com

Karen Reese Tunnell
1130 Piedmont Avenue, NE #603
Atlanta, GA 30309
www.karentunnell.com

Kathy Schattleitner
2674 Caribbean Drive
Grand Junction, CO 81506

Marjan Kluepfel
3019 Oyster Bay Avenue
Davis, CA 95616
www. marjankluepfel.com

Reta Budd
484467 Sweaburg Road, RR 1
Beachville, ON N0J 1A0
Canada

Wendy Kroeker
Box 484
Rosenort, MB R0G 1W0
Canada
www.wendykroeker.com

Photographers

Franklin Nored
3137 Alec Way
Grand Junction, CO 81504
fnored@bresnan.net

John Polak
116 Pleasant Street #408
Easthampton, MA 01027
www.johnpolakphotography.com

Photography Center of Atlanta
1790 Cheshire Bridge Road NE
Suite 114
Atlanta, GA 30324
(404) 872-7262
www.magicsilver.com

Sheila Dunbar
624 Highway 54
Cayuga, ON N0A 1F0
Canada

Products

Bo-Nash Bonding Powder
Bo-Nash (North America), Inc.
(253) 864-6365
www.bonash.com

Color Evaluator II
Cottage Mills LLC
800 South Division Street
Suite C
Waunakee, WI 53597
info@cottagemills.com
(608) 850-3660
www.cottagemills.com

Create-A-Pattern
Bosal Foam & Fiber
171 Washington Street
Limerick, ME 04048
info@bosalfoam.com
(800) 343-1818

Easy Pattern Tracing Cloth (45"
[114.3cm] wide)
Pellon Consumer Products
4801 Ulmerton Road
Clearwater, FL 33762
(800) 223-5275
www.pellonprojects.com

Steam-A-Seam
The Warm Company
5529 186th Place SW
Lynnwood, WA 98037
info@warmcompany.com
(800) 234- 9276

Sulky Super Solvy
Sulky of America
980 Cobb Place Blvd., Suite 130
Kennesaw, GA 30144
info@ sulky.com
(800) 874-4115

Wonder-Under
Pellon Consumer Products
4801 Ulmerton Road
Clearwater, FL 33762
(800) 223-5275
www.pellonprojects.com

fw

a content + ecommerce company

www.fwmedia.com

18 17 16 15   5 4 3

ISBN-13: 978-1-4402-3843-7
SRN: U7633

DISTRIBUTED IN CANADA BY FRASER DIRECT
100 Armstrong Avenue
Georgetown, ON, Canada L7G 5S4
Tel: (905) 877-4411

DISTRIBUTED IN THE U.K. AND EUROPE BY F+W MEDIA INTERNATIONAL
Brunel House, Newton Abbot, Devon, TQ12 4PU, England
Tel: (+44) 1626 323200, Fax: (+44) 1626 323319
Email: postmaster@davidandcharles.co.uk

DISTRIBUTED IN AUSTRALIA BY CAPRICORN LINK
P.O. Box 704, S. Windsotr NSW, 2756 Australia
Tel: (02) 4560 1600   Fax: 02 4577 5288
Email: books@capricornlink.com.au

Project managed by Noel Rivera
Edited by Kelly M. Biscopink
Designed by Kelly Pace
Production coordinated by Greg Nock
Photography by Al Parrish and OMS Photography

Metric Conversion Chart

To convert	to	multiply by
Inches	Centimeters	2.54
Centimeters	Inches	0.4
Feet	Centimeters	30.5
Centimeters	Feet	0.03
Yards	Meters	0.9
Meters	Yards	1.1

Cathy Geier is an award-winning quilter, author, teacher and lecturer who specializes in landscape quilts. She earned her bachelor of arts degree in art history from the University of Wisconsin, Madison, and sets up her landscapes with the eye of a painter who uses fabrics for her palette. Her quilts have been juried into national shows, won national and regional ribbons, and have been featured in *American Quilter*, *Quilter's Newsletter*, Fons & Porter's *Love of Quilting* and *Quilt World* magazines. She is the author of several articles and a book, *Watercolor Landscape Quilts* (Krause Publications). Cathy currently owns and manages Patchworks that Praise, an online quilt shop specializing in fabrics for landscape quilting.

Cathy invented and patented a new piecing technique using a tear-away foundation. This technique enables quilters to sew together multiple squares and half square triangles very quickly, easily and (most importantly) accurately. She then went on to adapt the method to sew strip-pieced and string-pieced landscapes.

Cathy is married with three grown children. Her husband's job with the US Forest Service has taken her family to some of the most scenic places in the country. Her love of the forests, mountains and lakes around her is reflected in her quilts.

Index

String Quilt Revival

by Virginia Baker, Barbara Sanders
    and Nancy Zieman

String quilts have been around for centuries, but in *String Quilt Revival*, this time-tested artform is given a new life! Learn how to sew a variety of string quilt blocks by following clear step-by-step instructions, and discover a new type of foundation: no-show mesh stabilizer, which minimizes distortion of the blocks and doesn't need to be removed. It's a no-fuss approach to quilting that's sure to become a favorite. This technique is perfect for both beginners and skilled quilters, and it produces beautiful results without the worry of precision piecing.

The Quilting Arts Book

by Patricia Bolton

Beginners and seasoned crafters alike will find inspiration and instruction in this definitive quilting resource that combines foundational techniques for quilting and fiber art with tips and tricks for creating one-of-a-kind works of art. Showcased here are some of the most popular topics, articles and artists from past issues of *Quilting Arts* magazine, as well as new and fresh methods from today's most respected contemporary quilt artists. Hands-on workshops introduce crafters to each facet of the art-quilt trade— from creating abstract, pictorial and landscape quilts to in-depth techniques on surface design and stitching applications.

GET MORE GREAT QUILTING IDEAS AT WWW.QUILTINGDAILY.COM!